"This book will be a truly helpful resource for those who struggle with worry. Written by two seasoned experts on the topic in clear and practical terms, *The Worry Workbook* will guide you through a series of therapeutic exercises based in the latest theory and science of worry and anxiety. It is a book for doing, rather than just for reading; but it's one that promises to provide relief from worry and anxiety to those who need it most."

—**Adam S. Radomsky, PhD**, professor of psychology at Concordia University,
and editor of *Journal of Behavior Therapy and Experimental Psychiatry*

"Most people worry from time to time. But for some, worry is a constant companion. It makes mountains out of molehills. It screams 'catastrophe!' where others seem to brush things off. It turns simple matters into agonizing predicaments, keeps you up at night when others are soundly asleep, and turns a relaxing day into knotted muscles. But is does not have to be this way. Robichaud and Buhr take decades of the leading research and clinical insights, and present them in a clear, easy-to-understand program to help you understand and overcome your anxiety. Don't worry!"

—**Peter Norton, PhD**, professor of clinical psychology at Monash University
in Australia, and director of the Monash FEAR Clinic

"Why do some people worry more than others? In this book, Melisa Robichaud and Kristin Buhr present a clear and simple explanation of worry. Their theory is based on twenty-five years of research on worry, anxiety, and intolerance of uncertainty. To my knowledge, this is the first self-help book to systematically address the relationships between uncertainty, perfectionism, and problem solving, and to do so without referring to a particular mental health problem. Moreover, Robichaud and Buhr present well-defined and concrete self-help strategies that are closely tied to recent theories of learning. By pointing out the key role of safety behaviors in worry, they have really 'hit the nail on the head.' If you are someone who struggles with worry, it is almost impossible that you will not benefit from the countless examples of self-help strategies listed in this book."

—**Michel Dugas, PhD**, clinical psychologist and professor of psychology at
the Université du Québec en Outaouais

"Drawn from strong scientific foundations, *The Worry Workbook* is a straightforward yet compelling tool for those suffering with worry and chronic anxiety. In prescribing experiments that paradoxically embrace uncertainty, Robichaud and Buhr provide a blueprint towards combating safety behaviors and promoting a fuller and more enriching life despite unpredictability in the world."

—**Douglas Mennin, PhD**, professor in the department of counseling and
clinical psychology at Teachers College, Columbia University

T0301214

# The
# Worry
# Workbook

CBT Skills to Overcome Worry & Anxiety

by Facing the Fear of Uncertainty

Melisa Robichaud, PhD | Kristin Buhr, PhD

New Harbinger Publications, Inc.

NEW HARBINGER PUBLICATIONS is a
registered trademark of New Harbinger Publications, Inc.

Distributed in Canada by Raincoast Books

Copyright © 2018 by Melisa Robichaud and Kristin Buhr
New Harbinger Publications, Inc.
5674 Shattuck Avenue
Oakland, CA 94609
www.newharbinger.com

Cover design by Amy Shoup

Edited by Cindy Nixon

Library of Congress Cataloging-in-Publication Data on file

Printed in the United States of America

24     23     22

10     9     8     7     6     5     4     3

To my dad, Jacques Robichaud

—M. R.


For Dan and Logan

—K. B.

# Contents

# Foreword
## by Martin M. Antony, PhD

Do you often find yourself wondering, *How can I possibly get all of my work done? There are not enough hours in the day!* or *How can I make sure that my children are safe when the world is such a dangerous place?* Do you find yourself predicting that catastrophe is around the corner—for example, *I'm going to fail my exam!* or *I will make a fool of myself if I speak up in meetings*? Do you ruminate about how to solve potential problems even before they happen? These are the sorts of experiences that are common when we worry.

We all worry—it's a normal part of life. At the same time, worry can be a problem if it happens too frequently or too intensely. Intense worry is associated with a fear of uncertainty, which many experts believe is at the core of the problem. Worry may also lead us to engage in behaviors that contribute to the problem over the long term, such as avoiding situations and experiences that trigger worry or relying too much on behaviors that make us feel safe. For example, if you worry excessively about what others think about you, you may avoid social situations or use "safety behaviors" (such as having a few glasses of wine or avoiding eye contact) whenever you have to be around other people. In addition, excessive worry is often associated with other issues, such as perfectionism, anxiety, depressed mood, difficulty making decisions, and difficulty solving problems.

*The Worry Workbook* is the first workbook to focus specifically on the experience of worry and fear of uncertainty across a wide range of problems. If you worry too much about many different things, then this book is for you. It's practical, straightforward, easy to read, and well informed by the latest scientific research on the nature and treatment of excessive worry. It will help you understand where your worry comes from and what causes it to continue over time. The exercises in this book will teach you to recognize patterns of thinking and behaving that contribute to worry, including fear of uncertainty and the excessive use of safety behaviors. More importantly, you will learn strategies for changing your worry.

The book focuses on the use of "behavioral experiments" to test out beliefs about uncertainty and the dangers associated with it. Most of us tend to assume that our beliefs are true. This book encourages the reader to think of worry-related thoughts as guesses or hypotheses rather than facts and to conduct experiments to discover the truth. Experiments provide firsthand experiences to reduce the fear of uncertainty, thereby decreasing the tendency to worry. By using these strategies, you will learn to evaluate the situations that trigger your worry in a more balanced, flexible, and realistic way.

After introducing core strategies for reducing worry and fear of uncertainty, the book provides detailed instruction on how to apply the treatment to a range of problems. You will learn how to combat worry in the context of anxiety-related disorders, including generalized anxiety disorder, social anxiety disorder, illness anxiety disorder, and obsessive-compulsive disorder. You will also learn to combat worry and fear of uncertainty in the context of excessive perfectionism and difficulties with decision making. The book concludes with a chapter on overcoming obstacles that may impact the success of your treatment and ensuring that your improvements are maintained over the long term.

To get the most out of this book, it will be important to set aside time to practice the strategies on a regular basis. Over time, you should notice an improvement in your worry, as well as associated problems with anxiety, perfectionism, and decision making.

Good luck on your journey toward a life with less worry!

# Introduction

If you're reading this book, you're probably looking for help to manage your worries. However, dealing with worries can be tricky: if you worry excessively, you've probably already tried a range of strategies, from distracting yourself or ignoring your worries to problem solving, thinking positively, or challenging your worries. Many people find that these strategies aren't all that helpful, and even if they are occasionally able to let go of worries, new ones can crop up. Our aim for this workbook, then, isn't to just provide tools to deal with specific worries as they pop up; rather, we want you to understand why you worry in the first place in order to tackle worry at its source.

Although we'll be encouraging you to approach your worries from a perspective that may seem new to you, the tools in this workbook are based on a well-established treatment approach that has undergone decades of research to prove its effectiveness. If you're going to put your time and energy into something, we think it's important to pick strategies that have been shown to work. Specifically, the strategies in this workbook are based on a treatment approach called *cognitive behavior therapy* (CBT), which is a type of psychological therapy that focuses on identifying problematic areas of your life and directly targeting what is maintaining them. This is achieved by focusing on the relationship between thoughts, behaviors, and emotions. In a nutshell, we know that changing what you do can lead to changes in your thoughts and feelings, just like changing how you think can lead to changes in your behaviors and feelings. Because of this, CBT involves learning strategies to identify and target behaviors and thoughts that are inadvertently maintaining the problem. The goal of this workbook is therefore to help you act and think in ways that will ultimately reduce your worries.

## Who Is This Book For?

This workbook is aimed at anyone who experiences problematic worry, regardless of what they worry about or how much they worry. We designed this book to be helpful if you experience mild bouts of worry or have been diagnosed with an anxiety disorder. It can help you tackle worries related to health, safety, social situations, work or school, relationships, and daily life, as well as problems with perfectionism and decision making. Although we wrote this workbook in a way that allows you to use it on your own, it can also be used with a CBT therapist who can guide you through it. Working with a therapist can be particularly beneficial if your symptoms are severe or you're struggling with a significant anxiety disorder.

# Are You Ready to Tackle Your Worries?

Because we want everyone who uses this workbook to have as much success as possible and see real change in their lives, we think it's important to make sure you're ready to begin tackling your worries. Although there's a lot of research demonstrating the effectiveness of CBT, not everyone who uses CBT will see results, and this may be due to the level of effort involved. Tackling worries involves learning new ways to think and act, which is an acquired skill. Like any skill, it requires practice to see real improvement. Let's say you wanted to learn to play the guitar, so you took weekly lessons for a few months. If you just went to your lesson each week but didn't practice between lessons, you probably wouldn't play that well. However, if you consistently practiced what you learned, you could expect to become a pretty good player. And if you continued to practice over time, you would likely see your ability continue to improve.

The same holds true for the CBT skills in this workbook. There are numerous exercises throughout the book, all designed to give you a better understanding of worry and help you practice and hopefully master the skills. If you don't complete the exercises regularly, you can expect to get some useful knowledge about worry (and perhaps even find that you worry a bit less), but you're unlikely to see any major changes in your overall worry. Because of this, we strongly encourage you to think about whether you're ready to put forth the effort necessary to tackle your worries. It's important that you wait until you're willing to put in the time and energy before starting this workbook. If you've made the decision to improve your quality of life by working on your worries, we hope you'll give yourself the best shot at succeeding.

# How to Use This Book

We recommend that you read through all the chapters in order, as each chapter builds on the information in the last. Go at your own pace and take as much time as you need to work through each chapter and the various exercises. Throughout the workbook, we've given you suggestions about how long to spend on each exercise and where you can find downloadable materials for them (at the website for this book: http://www.newharbinger.com/40064; see the very back of this book for more details). Feel free to spend more time on sections that are relevant to you and skip over parts that don't pertain to you. We recommend that you set aside a minimum of thirty to sixty minutes a week to read through the chapters and work on the exercises. Remember that learning to better manage your worry takes time. The more you put into it, the more you'll get out of it.

# When to Seek Professional Help

Learning to manage worry on your own can be challenging. If you've been diagnosed with or believe you have an anxiety disorder, the strategies presented in this workbook may not be sufficient to completely overcome the problem. If you find yourself struggling or having difficulty utilizing the strategies, consider seeking professional help. Talk to your family doctor and seek out a therapist who specializes in CBT. The good news is that even if you seek professional help, the strategies introduced in this workbook can provide a solid foundation for continuing to work on overcoming problematic worry.

# Moving Toward Change

If you've struggled with problematic worry, it can be hard to imagine a life without it. In fact, many people who describe themselves as "worriers" feel like worry is part of who they are. Worry and anxiety can seep into many aspects of life. They can control decisions, dictate actions, impact the ability to relax and enjoy things, lead to stress and exhaustion, interfere with work and school, and take a toll on relationships. But figuring out how to reduce excessive worry can lead to dramatic life changes. Imagine making choices based on what you want to do (not on what your anxiety "lets" you do), enjoying things, being able to relax and be spontaneous, and feeling productive in your life. This workbook can help you successfully overcome problematic worry and ultimately live a fuller and richer life.

# CHAPTER 1

# The Problem with Worry

Worry is a universal human experience. Everyone worries from time to time, especially during periods of stress. For example, it's completely normal to worry when you're awaiting the results of a medical test, taking an exam, or going to a job interview. Worry becomes a problem when it's happening so frequently that it starts interfering with your life. Having worries constantly spinning in your head can be overwhelming and exhausting. It can interfere with your ability to function at work or school, and it can negatively impact your relationships, as well as your ability to relax and enjoy life. In fact, worry is a common and impairing symptom present in most anxiety disorders (American Psychiatric Association [APA] 2013), although it can also be problematic if you don't have an anxiety disorder. If worry is bothering you and impacting your life, then this workbook is for you. Our goal is to help you better understand and manage your worries, regardless of what you worry about or how much you worry.

In this chapter, you'll develop a better understanding of what worry is and how it works, and you'll begin to identify your own worry fingerprint. Armed with this knowledge, you'll be ready to use the strategies described in later chapters to help you tackle excessive worry.

## What Is Worry?

Psychologists have debated for years how to properly define "worry"; however, a good working definition is that worry is a chain of thoughts. In other words, worry occurs in the mind: when we worry, we are thinking about negative events that might occur in the future. It turns out that when we worry, we are actually engaged in two separate but related thought processes (Robichaud and Dugas 2015).

The first worry process involves thoughts about all the possible things that could go wrong in a situation. Let's say you have to cancel dinner plans with a friend because you don't feel well. You might think, *What if my friend doesn't believe I'm not feeling well and thinks I'm just canceling for no good reason? He might get angry with me and tell other people I'm not a good friend because I cancel plans at the last minute. Or what if he says that he doesn't mind rescheduling to another day, but he's actually upset with me and doesn't want to be friends anymore?* This first part of worry involves thinking about *worst-case scenarios* or *catastrophic outcomes*, which in this example include your friend being angry with you and ending the friendship.

The second thought process involves *mental problem solving.* Here, we attempt to plan for or prevent our feared negative outcomes. Using the previous example, you might think, *I could take the time to explain to my friend how sick I've been feeling all day, and I could reschedule our dinner plans right away so he doesn't think I don't want to see him. I could also call him the next day to make sure he isn't upset with me.* Each of these attempts at mental problem solving involves trying to develop a plan to manage the potential catastrophic outcomes you've thought of.

Taking these parts of worry together, worry involves *mentally planning and preparing for future events* by thinking about all the possible negative outcomes that might occur and attempting to problem solve those outcomes in advance.

## How Is Worry Different from Anxiety?

Before we discuss worry in greater detail, it's a good idea to first explain the difference between "worry" and "anxiety." These terms are often used interchangeably, and although they are related processes, they are actually distinct. Whereas worry takes place in the mind, anxiety takes place in the body. Anxiety involves a host of physical sensations we all experience when feeling threatened or in danger, including a racing heart, stomach distress, sweating, shaking, shortness of breath, numbness or tingling sensations, and feelings of light-headedness, dizziness, or even a sense of depersonalization. The more anxious we get, the more intense these sensations can feel.

Feeling anxious can be uncomfortable and unpleasant, but it's not dangerous. In fact, anxiety is a survival mechanism present in all living creatures. It's sometimes referred to as the "fight-or-flight response": whenever we feel threatened in some way, anxiety helps us deal with danger by activating the body and preparing us to either fight or run away (flight) from whatever is threatening us. Worry, on the other hand, involves *thinking about* threats or dangers that might potentially occur. Since anxiety is the body's response to threat, anxiety can be triggered by worries. In other words, anxiety is the *result* of worry. Because of this, learning how to manage your worries will also help you reduce feelings of anxiety.

Although anxiety is a system in the body designed to help us cope with danger, there are two major problems with anxiety that explain why worry can trigger our body's fight-or-flight system. First, anxiety doesn't distinguish between threats where you're in actual physical danger and nonphysical threats. If you're afraid of public speaking, for example, you're likely to feel anxious when giving a speech. You might be worried you'll do a bad job, forget what you want to say, or look or sound odd in front of others. Though your worries in this situation might seem threatening, you probably don't think that you're in actual physical danger. For instance, you don't expect anyone to throw bricks at you while giving your speech. The problem is that anxiety won't make that distinction. Because you're feeling threatened by the possibility of doing a bad job and potentially being embarrassed, your fight-or-flight system mobilizes your body's responses to physical threat. This can be less than helpful when the danger is not a physical threat: sweating, trembling, and having a racing heart are unhelpful sensations when giving a speech.

Another problem with anxiety is that it doesn't go off when we *are* in danger, but rather when we *think* we're in danger. This means that whenever you think that a situation is threatening, you're likely to experience anxiety even if the situation isn't actually threatening. Let's say you hear a noise and think someone is breaking into your home—that threatening thought will automatically lead to anxiety. However, the noise you heard might have been a tree branch scratching against the window. Your anxiety in the moment occurred because you *perceived* a danger, not because there actually was a danger. In other words, anxiety is not a "danger detector." So feeling anxious doesn't mean that there is an actual threat present; it means that you feel threatened in the moment.

A good way to think about anxiety is as the body's smoke detector. Smoke detectors don't go off when there is a fire; they go off when there's smoke. A smoke detector can go off when there is a real fire, but it can also go off if you burn a piece of toast. Just like you can have a false alarm with a smoke detector, you can also have a false alarm with anxiety.

## Understanding the Worry Cycle

As explained earlier, worry involves mentally planning and preparing for future events: when we worry, we're mentally anticipating potential threats and trying to prepare for them ahead of time. However, worry can easily become an exhaustive process because there is an infinite number of things you can imagine going wrong, and your mind can repeatedly replay those scenarios. This process of getting caught up in worries can be understood as a *worry cycle,* and it involves several components. A visual illustration is presented in figure 1.1.

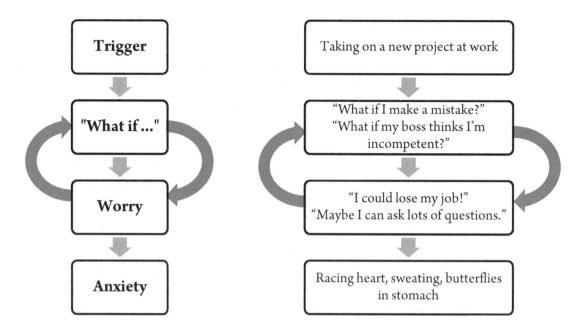

Figure 1.1: The Worry Cycle

We may not be aware of it, but there is always some sort of *trigger* that sets off worries. Triggers can be either external or internal. External triggers involve any outside event or situation that is actually occurring, whereas internal triggers are thoughts or physical sensations that are occurring in your body or mind. Triggers lead to an initial *what-if question* that sets off the worry cycle.

Here are some sample triggers and the initial what-if questions that might result.

### External Triggers

- Receiving an invitation to a new restaurant: *What if I don't like the food?*

- Leaving the house: *What if I forgot to turn off the stove?*

- Taking an exam: *What if I fail?*

### Internal Triggers

- Thinking about buying new sneakers: *What if I get a pair of sneakers and find a better pair later on?*

- Thinking about applying for a new job: *What if I get the job and I hate it?*

- Realizing that you forgot something: *What if my memory loss is a sign of Alzheimer's?*

After a trigger sets off a what-if question, the process of *worry* begins. When we worry, we're thinking about negative events that have *not yet happened* (and may not happen), so there are endless possibilities about what *could* happen and how you *might* deal with it. Because of this, worrying often leads to more what-if questions and, subsequently, more worries. Let's say Sarah was given a new project to complete at work (trigger), which leads her to think, *What if I make a mistake?* (initial what-if question). Sarah's worries might include: *I could completely ruin the project, make my boss angry, and even get fired! Maybe I could ask for help from my colleagues or make sure to ask my boss lots of questions beforehand so I don't make any mistakes.*

The problem is that Sarah doesn't know what obstacles, if any, she might encounter while completing the project, so the possibilities for what could happen are endless, as are the possibilities for things that might go wrong. As such, Sarah is likely to have more what-if thoughts that set off more worries about different topics. She might think, *What if my boss gets annoyed at me for asking questions, or what if I make mistakes even after asking for clarification on the project? My boss might think I'm incompetent and fire me. I could probably work extra hard on this project and volunteer to take on new tasks to show what a good employee I am. But what if she fires me anyway? What if I can't find another job and I'm unable to pay my bills!* It is easy to get caught in a worry cycle where what-if thoughts lead to more worries, which in turn lead to more what-if thoughts and even more worries.

These what-if thoughts and worries lead to feelings of *anxiety*. As mentioned earlier, because the negative scenarios we think about when we worry are threatening, they trigger the anxiety system. For Sarah, her worries are all threatening thoughts that would cause anxiety.

Although the worry cycle can be easy to understand, it's quite tricky to identify within yourself. For one thing, it's difficult to actually "catch" your thoughts in the moment. Think of your thoughts and feelings in a worry cycle like a washing machine: just as it's difficult to see individual items while the washing machine is spinning, it can be difficult to catch individual thoughts spinning in your mind.

It's also challenging to identify patterns or reoccurring themes to your worry. That's because our memory for past events isn't always good. For example, you probably remember what you had for dinner yesterday. But you might not recall what you had for dinner two weeks ago, and if you had to guess, you might think about what you usually have for dinner or what you had recently. Similarly, when you try to recall your worries over the past several days, you're largely guessing about the content of your worries, making it difficult to identify patterns or themes.

The best way to recognize any kind of pattern in your life, from what you tend to eat to what you typically worry about, is to write it down. This will give you a more accurate account of what you worry about, since you don't have to rely on your memory or best guesses. With this in mind, the following exercise will help you gather information about your worry patterns by recording your worries across an entire week. Throughout this workbook, we will often encourage you to write things down when completing an exercise to ensure that you're capturing an accurate record of your experience.

# EXERCISE 1.1:
## Tracking Your Worries

One of the best ways to "catch" your worries is to use anxiety as a cue. When you notice feelings of anxiety, stop and ask yourself what's going on (trigger) and what you're thinking about (what-if questions/worries), then record that information on the worry tracking worksheet below, along with the date and time and the level of anxiety you're feeling on a scale of 0 to 10.

You don't need to write down every single worry related to a specific trigger; instead, try to identify the initial what-if question and one or two subsequent worries. Nor do you need to fill out this sheet more than three times a day. This isn't meant to be an exhaustive list of all your worries, but rather a slice of life to help you develop a picture of your own worry patterns.

An example of a completed sheet is provided here, as well as a blank sheet for your own use. (A PDF of this worksheet is available at http://www.newharbinger.com/40064.)

| Date/Time | Trigger | "What if…?"/Worries | Anxiety (0 to 10) |
|---|---|---|---|
| Wednesday 9 a.m. | Headache since waking up this morning | What if this is a symptom of a serious disease? I could have cancer or a brain tumor. | 8 |
| Wednesday 2 p.m. | Received a text from a friend asking for my opinion about what computer to buy | What if I give her bad advice? She could be furious at me for suggesting that she buy a terrible computer. | 5 |
| Wednesday 9 p.m. | Thinking about the meeting tomorrow at work | What if I say something stupid? My boss could fire me, and I would be humiliated. | 6 |

| Date/Time | Trigger | "What if…?"/Worries | Anxiety (0 to 10) |
|-----------|---------|---------------------|-------------------|
|           |         |                     |                   |
|           |         |                     |                   |
|           |         |                     |                   |
|           |         |                     |                   |
|           |         |                     |                   |
|           |         |                     |                   |

# Identifying Your Worry Fingerprint

Although everybody worries, we don't all worry about the same things. What sets off a worry cycle for one person might not be a concern for someone else. Because of this, it's a good idea to understand what types of situations are most likely to lead to worry for you. In essence, you need to obtain information to recognize your own unique worry fingerprint. This is particularly important since the strategies for managing worry that you'll learn in this workbook will sometimes differ depending on what you worry about.

If you completed exercise 1.1 for at least one week, you hopefully have some good examples of your worry pattern. With this information, you can start identifying themes that come up most often for you. This next exercise will help you identify your worry fingerprint.

---

## EXERCISE 1.2:
## What Is Your Worry Fingerprint?

Listed below are a number of statements that relate to daily life worries. Read through the examples provided under each life area and provide a number from 1 to 3 indicating how typical the statement is of you. Use your responses from exercise 1.1 to help you identify your most frequent worry topics.

**Scoring:**

1 = Not typical of me

2 = Somewhat typical of me

3 = Very typical of me

### Health/Physical Symptoms

_____ I worry when I experience physical symptoms (headaches, stomachaches, minor aches or pains) that don't have a clear explanation as to why they occurred.

_____ I worry that minor changes in my physical health (being more tired one day, experiencing mild back pain, or experiencing light-headedness on occasion) might be symptoms of a serious illness (such as AIDS, cancer, brain tumor).

_____ I worry about contracting a disease (such as SARS, Zika virus) when traveling to different countries.

_____ I get quite concerned going for medical tests because I don't know how things will turn out.

## Danger/Safety

_____ I worry about natural disasters (earthquakes, hurricanes, tsunamis).

_____ I worry a lot about not being properly prepared if a disaster or crisis occurred.

_____ I often worry about being mugged or attacked when I'm walking alone.

_____ I'm often concerned about being involved in an accident (car crash or plane crash) when traveling.

_____ I worry about my house being broken into.

## Social Situations

_____ I'm worried about giving my opinions on things (such as movies or politics) when I don't know how others will react to what I have to say.

_____ I worry a lot about saying or doing the wrong thing when talking to new people.

_____ I don't like being responsible for any decision (where and when to meet, what to do) when out with friends.

_____ I have difficulty saying no to others.

_____ I frequently worry that I offended someone.

_____ I spend a lot of time worrying about what people think of me.

## Work/School

_____ I worry a lot about making mistakes or falling behind on tasks at work.

_____ I am often worried about what my boss thinks of me and whether I will be fired.

_____ I spend a lot of time thinking about the best way to complete tasks at work.

_____ I worry a lot about failing my exams or a course at school.

_____ When I'm doing homework, I'm often concerned that I won't understand the material or keep up with my schoolwork.

## Interpersonal Relationships

_____ I'm frequently concerned about the health of my family members.

_____ I worry my spouse might leave me one day.

_____ When my children are out, I worry that something bad might happen to them.

_____ I often worry about upsetting my friends.

## Daily Activities and Responsibilities

_____ I worry that I didn't lock my door or turn off all the appliances in my home.

_____ When I walk by something that I find potentially dangerous (needles, garbage), I worry about getting sick if I'm not completely sure I didn't step on it.

_____ When I am out, I worry I might lose my keys, wallet, or phone.

_____ Whenever I go somewhere new, I worry that I might get lost or have trouble finding parking.

_____ I worry about getting places on time due to unexpected events.

_____ I don't like when plans change unexpectedly.

Any other types of situations or themes that you worry about?

_____

_____

_____

All of the worry topics listed are now presented below. Place a check next to each one for which your scores were mostly 2 or 3.

_____ Health/Physical Symptoms

_____ Danger/Safety

_____ Social Situations

_____ Work/School

_____ Interpersonal Relationships

_____ Daily Activities and Responsibilities

This information will be important as you move through this workbook, since it will guide you toward the worry management strategies that will be most helpful to you. If your worries don't specifically fit into a listed theme, that's okay; the strategies in this workbook apply to all types of worries.

# When Is Worry a Problem?

Although everyone worries from time to time, problematic worry is something entirely different. In general, worry is a problem when it meets three criteria (APA 2013): First, worry is problematic when it's frequent, since the more time spent worrying, the more troubling it is likely to be. Second, problematic worry is excessive—that is, it's more frequent than the situation warrants or greater than what others might experience. Let's say you're worrying a lot about your job; it would be excessive if there were no significant issues or difficulties at work and if you or your loved ones thought you were worrying too much about it. However, if there were recent layoffs and you were told that you might be losing your job, then your worries would be considered appropriate given the situation. Third, worry is problematic if it's causing you significant distress and interfering with your life in some way.

Unfortunately, there are many ways that problematic worry can impact your life. Constant worry impairs your ability to concentrate or pay attention, it can be stressful and exhausting, and it interferes with your ability to relax. Excessive worry can also put a strain on your relationships, prevent you from being in the moment, and stop you from truly enjoying life.

## Worry and Anxiety Disorders

When worry causes significant distress or interference in someone's life, it might be indicative of a mental health problem. There are a number of anxiety disorders for which worry is a significant feature:

- Generalized anxiety disorder (GAD): Individuals with GAD worry excessively about daily life events (finances, work/school, health, family, the future). Excessive worry about everyday things is the primary symptom of this disorder.

- Social anxiety disorder (SAD): The main feature of SAD is excessive fear and avoidance of social situations where one might be judged or evaluated negatively. People with SAD worry about interacting in groups, with strangers, or with authority figures; saying no to requests; giving an opinion; or potentially displeasing others.

- Obsessive-compulsive disorder (OCD): There are two main features of OCD: *obsessions,* which are unwanted intrusive thoughts that cause anxiety, and *compulsions,* which are deliberate behaviors or mental acts performed to reduce anxiety and address obsessions. There are many different types of obsessions and compulsions that people can experience; however, doubt is a common worry theme present in OCD. For example, people with OCD commonly worry about whether they locked the door, came into contact with a potential contaminant, or accidentally harmed others (such as forgetting to wipe a wet spot on the floor that someone later slips on).

- Illness anxiety disorder (IAD): Also known as "health anxiety," IAD involves an excessive fear of having, or developing, a serious disease. People with IAD tend to worry that minor changes in their health are symptoms of a more serious medical problem.

Regardless of whether or not you've been diagnosed with an anxiety disorder, or whether your worries fit into one of these diagnoses, this workbook is for you! This is because not everyone with problematic worry has an anxiety disorder. Worry exists along a continuum, and people with anxiety disorders fall on the extreme end of the worry continuum. Moreover, not everyone worries about the same things. Whereas some people struggle with significant worries about one particular topic, others worry about a number of different issues. Wherever you fall on the worry continuum and whatever your worry fingerprint looks like, if worry is causing you problems, it can be extremely helpful to learn effective strategies to help you manage worry and anxiety in the long term.

## When Worry Is Not a Problem

As important as it is to recognize when worry is a problem that requires attention, it's also important to know when worry is appropriate and not a problem that needs fixing. In general, feelings of anxiety, sadness, and distress are normal emotions that occur from time to time and are part of the full spectrum of human experience. Life is fraught with stressors: important people in our lives can become ill, we can experience financial difficulties or job loss, and we sometimes undergo major life changes, such as moving, getting married, or having children. These situations are all stressful and are expected to increase worry and feelings of anxiety. Normal worries tend to be more temporary than problematic worries, decreasing in frequency or disappearing altogether once the stressor has passed.

Because worry is part of the normal human experience, it can be helpful to take some time to look at your worries (you can use your worry tracking sheet from exercise 1.1 for this) and determine whether they are appropriate given what's going on in your life right now. Questions to ask yourself include:

- *Do I worry about these topics only when there is significant stress going on in that area of my life?*

- *When there are no major stressors in my life, do I still worry a lot?*

- *Do I think I worry too much?*

- *Have other people told me I worry too much?*

If you worry only when faced with significant stressors, and if neither you nor others see your worry as excessive, then it's probably normal. If, on the other hand, you worry a lot even when there are no major stressors in your life, and if you or others think you worry too much, then worry is likely a problem for you. It's important to know that the goal of this workbook is to give you tools to manage your worries, not eliminate them. And even if you successfully use the strategies you'll learn in this book, you will still worry sometimes, since some level of worry is normal, especially during times of stress. However, learning to manage excessive worry can help you live a more fulfilling and enjoyable life.

# In a Nutshell

The aim of this chapter was to help you better understand worry, as well as identify your own unique worry fingerprint so you can begin addressing problematic worry. Here are some key points:

- Worry is a series of thoughts involving two related processes: (1) thinking about worst-case scenarios and catastrophic outcomes, and (2) a mental attempt to problem solve these negative scenarios.

- Worry is distinct from anxiety: whereas worry involves thoughts about potential threats or danger in the future, anxiety is the body's physical response to perceived threats.

- Worry can be a self-reinforcing cycle: the worry cycle starts with a trigger setting off a "what-if question," which in turn leads to worry and then anxiety. Because worry is a mental attempt to plan and prepare for potential negative outcomes, there are infinite possibilities of what could happen, thereby leading to more what-if questions and worries.

- Everyone has a distinct set of worries, which we call a "worry fingerprint." To understand your own worry fingerprint, record your worries for at least a week, then identify the most common worry themes you experience.

- Worry and anxiety are normal human experiences that occur from time to time, especially during times of stress. Problematic worry tends to be more frequent and excessive, leading to significant distress and interference.

Now that you're armed with more knowledge about *what* worry is, the next chapter will introduce *why* some people worry more than others. It might surprise you to discover that your reaction to the uncertainties of life plays a strong part in getting the engine of worry going—and keeping it going.

CHAPTER 2

# Why Do We Worry?

Regardless of what you worry about or how much you worry, an important step in coping with worry is understanding its relationship to an ever-present aspect of daily life: uncertainty. A great deal of psychological research has tied the fear, or intolerance, of uncertainty to worry (Dugas et al. 1998; Ladouceur et al. 2000; Meeten et al. 2012). The more people worry, the more they report being intolerant of uncertainty (Freeston et al. 1994), and this fear of uncertainty has been linked to a number of anxiety disorders, including generalized anxiety disorder (Dugas et al. 1995; Dugas, Marchand, and Ladouceur 2005), social anxiety disorder (Boelen and Reijntjes 2009), obsessive-compulsive disorder (Tolin et al. 2003), and illness anxiety disorder (Boelen and Carleton 2012). In fact, recent studies have suggested that fear of the unknown is a fundamental fear underlying both anxiety disorders and the experience of anxiety in general (Carleton 2016).

But life is filled with uncertainty, and when we worry about the uncertainties of life, there's always something to worry about. For example, we can't be completely sure we'll be on time for work or that we're getting the best deal on airline tickets for an upcoming vacation. We can never be completely certain of the outcome for any situation in life. Although most people are uncomfortable with uncertainty to some degree, some of us find uncertainty quite threatening and, as a result, worry excessively.

In this chapter, you'll learn about intolerance of uncertainty and its role in fueling worry, as well as why some people fear uncertainty more than others. You'll also learn how your thoughts play a huge role in the fear of uncertainty and how changing how you think can reduce worry in the long term.

## Understanding the Fear of Uncertainty

Before we can discuss the fear of uncertainty in daily life, we first need to be clear about what makes a particular situation uncertain. In general, any situation in which you are not 100 percent sure of the outcome can be deemed uncertain. This of course can include a wide range of situations.

In everyday life, however, uncertain situations typically fall into one of three categories (Inglis 2000; Lee 2001):

1. *Novel situations:* Any situation or event that's new or unfamiliar to us is necessarily uncertain. Going to a new restaurant, meeting new people, or attending a new exercise class are all situations where you aren't exactly sure what's going to happen because you've never been in that situation before.

2. *Ambiguous situations:* Some situations are uncertain because the situation itself is not entirely clear or well defined, making it difficult to know what to expect. For example, your boss telling you she wants to talk to you about the new project you're working on is pretty ambiguous, as it's not clear what she wants to talk about—she might want to tell you she's impressed with your work so far, she might simply want an update on your progress, or she might tell you she has major concerns about the project. There is uncertainty about both the nature of the situation (what your boss wants to talk to you about) and the outcome (whether it will be positive, negative, or neutral).

3. *Unpredictable situations:* Some situations are uncertain because there's no way to predict exactly what will happen. You don't know for sure what will happen when you take an exam, for instance. You can study very hard for it, but you won't know exactly what questions you'll be asked until you actually take the exam.

As you may have noticed, these types of uncertain situations are scenarios we all experience every day, yet we react to them with varying levels of fear and discomfort. While some of us struggle with the uncertainty in these situations, others seem able to handle it with ease. In the next section, we'll discuss why.

## Intolerance of Uncertainty and Worry

Not everyone reacts to uncertainty the same way. Some people get very upset or anxious at mild levels of uncertainty in daily life, some don't mind dealing with a bit of uncertainty, and others even enjoy not knowing what will happen. Because of this, different people encountering the same uncertain situation will have very different reactions to that situation, ranging from fear to indifference to pleased anticipation or excitement.

The difference in reaction has to do with how fearful, or *intolerant,* a person is of uncertainty. *Intolerance of uncertainty* refers to the way people think about uncertain situations. People who are highly intolerant of uncertainty tend to view uncertain situations as negative, stressful, and upsetting situations that are difficult to manage and should be avoided (Buhr and Dugas 2002).

So how does our intolerance of uncertainty affect worry? In chapter 1, we defined worry as a mental attempt to plan and prepare for any eventuality: when we worry, we are thinking about all the worst-case scenarios that might occur, as well as attempting to mentally problem solve those potential negative outcomes. In essence, we are trying to reduce or minimize the uncertainty of daily life situations by anticipating what *could* happen and how we might cope with it. Therefore, the more threatened we are by uncertainty, the more we're likely to worry.

A good way to understand intolerance of uncertainty is as an allergy. When you're allergic to something, you usually have a strong reaction when exposed to even small amounts of that particular allergen. If you're allergic to cats, you might sneeze and get red, watery eyes when around one. Similarly, if you're someone who is intolerant of uncertainty, you are likely to have a strong reaction to even a small amount of uncertainty in daily life: you might worry a lot about the situation and feel anxious, distressed, or annoyed.

## The Continuum of Intolerance of Uncertainty

Given that there is always the possibility that an uncertain situation can turn out negatively, it makes sense that most everyone struggles to some degree with tolerating uncertainty. We all generally prefer some predictability in our lives, and we're likely to experience some worry and anxiety the more uncertain a situation becomes. However, intolerance of uncertainty exists on a continuum, and people can therefore differ a great deal in their level of uncertainty tolerance (Dugas and Robichaud 2006).

If you're someone who can decide where to go on holidays by simply going to the airport and seeing what flights look interesting that day, or pick up and move to a new city without securing a job or a place to live beforehand, then you're probably someone with a high tolerance for uncertainty. If, instead, you're someone who always goes to the exact same restaurant because you already know that you like it, or you always leave extra early for appointments to ensure that you're on time, then you are probably someone with a low tolerance for uncertainty. Because your intolerance, or fear, of uncertainty affects how much you worry on a daily basis, it can be helpful to figure out where you are on the continuum of uncertainty tolerance. The following exercise will help you determine this.

## EXERCISE 2.1:
## Are You Intolerant of Uncertainty?

Read over the following statements and provide a number from 1 to 3 indicating how typical the statement is of you.

**Scoring:**

1 = Not typical of me

2 = Somewhat typical of me

3 = Very typical of me

1. _____ I tend to assume the worst will happen when faced with a situation in which I am unsure of the outcome.

2. _____ I feel that unexpected events can ruin everything.

3. _____ I think I will fall apart if a situation turns out badly and I wasn't able to plan for it.

4. _____ It bothers me when I don't know how things will turn out.

5. _____ I get anxious and stressed when I'm in an uncertain situation.

6. _____ I get frustrated when I don't have all the information I need.

7. _____ I have a hard time making decisions.

8. _____ I often look for a lot of information or do a lot of research before making a decision.

9. _____ I sometimes question decisions I've already made because I'm no longer certain I made the right decision.

10. _____ I don't like surprises.

11. _____ I like to plan out my day in great detail.

12. _____ I prefer to keep a very predictable routine.

13. _____ I get frustrated whenever there is a change in plans.

14. _____ I tend to avoid situations when I'm not sure how they will turn out.

If you scored a 2 or 3 on at least seven of the above statements, you likely have some intolerance to uncertainty. In general, the more items that you scored as either somewhat or very typical of you, the higher your intolerance of uncertainty.

# The Influence of Beliefs About Uncertainty

The reason why some situations are more difficult to tolerate than others actually has less to do with the situation itself and more to do with what a person *thinks* about the situation. This is closely related to one's intolerance for uncertainty. Research shows that if you're highly intolerant of uncertainty,

Why Do We Worry?

you're more likely to interpret uncertain situations as threatening and anticipate a negative outcome (Koerner and Dugas 2008; Oglesby et al. 2016). As such, if you have a high intolerance for uncertainty, you probably have *negative beliefs* about the consequences of an uncertain situation.

To illustrate, let's say Neil's friend unexpectedly invites him to spend the weekend at her cabin with a group of friends. This is an uncertain situation: Neil has never been to the cabin, and since Neil's friend asked him unexpectedly, he doesn't have much time to plan for the trip. How Neil reacts to this invitation will depend on his beliefs about the uncertainty of this situation. If he has a fairly high tolerance for uncertainty, he might be excited at the prospect of staying with friends, going fishing and canoeing, or having a campfire at night. However, if Neil is very intolerant of uncertainty, this sudden trip could be very anxiety-provoking: he might worry about finding the place, whether everyone would get along, or if spending a whole weekend in a cabin would be boring.

## Negative Beliefs About Uncertainty

As you can see from the cabin trip example, our thoughts can influence how we react to a situation just as much as what is actually happening in the situation itself. So what kind of thoughts would lead us to view an uncertain situation as threatening? There are three major negative beliefs about uncertainty and its consequences that influence how we will react in novel, ambiguous, and unpredictable situations (Birrell et al. 2011; Sexton and Dugas 2009).

### Belief #1: Uncertain events will have negative outcomes

Although the outcomes of uncertain events are by their very nature unsure (since they haven't happened yet), some of us are more likely to expect that the outcomes will be negative. For example, if you're going to a job interview, you might assume that you won't get the job, or if you're trying out a new exercise class, you might expect that the class will be too hard and you won't be able to keep up.

### Belief #2: Negative outcomes will be catastrophic

Not only do some of us expect uncertain situations to turn out negatively, but we also tend to anticipate that the outcome will be horrible. Let's say you aren't sure whether you locked the front door before you left the house this morning. When you expect uncertain situations to be catastrophic, you might believe that not only did you leave the door unlocked (that is, the uncertain situation turned out negatively), but that your house will be broken into and robbed. If we have this negative belief about uncertainty, we're more likely to think that the "worst-case scenario" will actually occur.

## *Belief #3*: You'll be unable to cope with negative outcomes

The third negative belief is the expectation that when an uncertain situation turns out negatively, we'll be unable to deal with the outcome. For example, if you're going to visit a friend's home and you're unfamiliar with the location, you might expect to get lost (negative outcome) because of the uncertainty of how to get there. However, if you believe that you're unable to cope with negative outcomes, you might also expect that when you get lost, you won't know what to do: perhaps you'll be overwhelmed with fear and anxiety and have no idea how to get your bearings and find your friend's house.

It makes sense that if we expect uncertain situations to turn out negatively and to be unable to cope with those negative outcomes, then daily life situations become very threatening and leave us feeling worried and anxious whenever we are faced with uncertainty. However, given that life is filled with uncertainty, having these negative beliefs leads to excessive worry and anxiety, which is stressful and exhausting and can make everyday life feel overwhelming.

Furthermore, we might not realize how these beliefs significantly impact the choices we make. Many people who fear uncertainty tend to hold the belief "Better the devil you know than the devil you don't"—in other words, it's better to stick with what is familiar than to try out things that are new or uncertain. But this can mean missing out on opportunities that could enrich life. For example, you might stay at a job you don't like because you're worried that the search for a more interesting and enjoyable job could be unsuccessful, or you might avoid committing to a romantic relationship because you're not completely sure how it will turn out. Looking at the world this way can take the pleasure and spontaneity out of life and make it seem very scary. Holding negative beliefs about uncertainty ultimately robs us of being able to live a full life.

## *Balanced Beliefs About Uncertainty*

So what kind of beliefs can make the uncertainty in daily life situations less threatening? Many people think that the alternative is to look at uncertainty in a positive light; that is, to expect that uncertain situations will always turn out well. As nice as it might be to think like this, it's not always realistic. The reality is that negative things do happen sometimes: you can get lost when driving to a new location or forget to lock the front door when leaving the house. Always expecting a positive outcome can leave you feeling overwhelmed and frustrated when things sometimes turn out negatively.

The most basic element of an uncertain situation is that you don't know what will happen. Therefore, a healthier perspective is to hold a *balanced* or neutral view about the outcome, without the expectation that things will necessarily turn out poorly (or positively). For each of the three negative beliefs about uncertainty, there is a corresponding balanced belief—one that leaves room for positive, negative, and neutral outcomes for any uncertain situation and views uncertainty as less threatening overall.

## *Balanced belief #1:* Uncertain situations will probably turn out all right

Because we don't know what the outcome of an uncertain situation will be, a balanced perspective would be to assume that it should turn out all right provided there is no evidence to the contrary. Let's say that you're starting your first day at a new job. This is an uncertain situation, since you haven't worked at this job before and don't know what to expect. A balanced belief might be to expect that everything should go relatively fine. Having a balanced perspective doesn't mean you expect your first day to be great; since you don't know how it will go, there's no reason to think it'll be great, but there's also no reason to expect it to go badly. If you think about uncertain situations from this more neutral and realistic perspective, you're less likely to feel threatened.

## *Balanced belief #2:* If the outcome is negative, it probably won't be catastrophic

As mentioned earlier, uncertain situations can indeed have a negative outcome. However, without evidence, there is no reason to believe that the negative outcome will inevitably involve the worst-case scenario. Rather, a more balanced perspective would assume that any negative outcome will likely be more of a hassle than a horror. Let's say you ordered something new at a restaurant. This is an uncertain situation, since you'll be eating a meal you've never tasted before and you don't know whether you'll like it. If you hold balanced beliefs, you might expect that the meal will probably taste fine, but even if you didn't like it, it wouldn't be catastrophic. That is, potentially not liking the meal you ordered is a hassle, but it's not horrible: you could order something else or get a bite to eat later. From this perspective, while the worst-case scenario in an uncertain situation is certainly possible, it's more likely that a negative outcome will be an inconvenience or a minor problem instead of a catastrophe.

## *Balanced belief #3:* If the outcome is negative, it will probably be manageable

The third balanced belief about uncertainty is the expectation that if a negative outcome does occur, it will likely be an outcome that can be handled. For example, if you're driving to your friend's place and get lost (negative outcome), you might believe that you'll probably be able to figure out where you are and eventually get to her place. Yet again, a balanced perspective on uncertain situations is not that everything will necessarily be positive, but rather that negative outcomes are most likely manageable when they do occur.

When we hold balanced beliefs about uncertainty, we're generally less fearful of uncertain situations because we're less likely to interpret them as threatening. As a result, we're less likely to be worried and anxious when faced with them. This means that the decisions we make in our life can be based on actual choice rather than fear. Let's say you're invited to a party where there will be several people you've never met. If you hold balanced beliefs about uncertainty, you might think that you'll probably get along with most people there, and even if you don't, you can handle it (perhaps by spending more time with the people you already know). With this perspective, you're probably not afraid to go to the party. However, you might decide that you just aren't in the mood for a party. Because you're not threatened by the party, your decision is based on your actual preference and not based on what your fears are "allowing" you to do.

In addition, by being less threatened by uncertainty, you're less likely to avoid novel, ambiguous, and unpredictable situations, which then allows you to find out what the actual outcome in those situations would be. For example, if you hold balanced beliefs about the party, you're more likely to give yourself the opportunity to see that maybe it turned out fine or it was actually a positive experience where you made new friends. Given the toll that worry and anxiety can take on us, along with the opportunities we miss out on when we hold negative beliefs about uncertainty, developing balanced beliefs about uncertainty can greatly enhance our lives. Before you're able to start working on your beliefs about uncertainty, though, you first need to know when they're triggered.

# Understanding Intolerance of Uncertainty Triggers

Because our beliefs have a strong influence on our reaction to uncertain situations, this means that it is not uncertain situations *per se* that are threatening. That is, we don't worry about uncertain situations because they are inherently threatening or dangerous. Rather, we worry about uncertain situations when they trigger our negative beliefs about uncertainty, which in turn lead us to anticipate a negative outcome that we'll be unable to handle.

However, just as some people are allergic to several things and not everyone has the same type of allergies, not everyone is intolerant of the same uncertain situations or to the same degree. You might find that you don't mind some types of uncertain situations but that others are really distressing. You might love surprises or enjoy traveling to new and exotic destinations, for instance, but you really don't like not knowing what other people think about you or whether you completed your tasks at work correctly. This explains why two people can be in the exact same uncertain situation and yet have very different reactions to it.

Let's use the example of Neil's invitation to the cabin for the weekend and assume that his friend Sabrina was also invited. Whereas Neil has negative beliefs about the uncertainty of social situations, Sabrina does not. As such, although both Neil and Sabrina would likely view the prospect of staying at a cabin with others as an uncertain social situation, only Neil would be anxious and worry excessively about it, as this situation would trigger his negative beliefs about uncertainty and therefore be viewed as threatening. But Sabrina would likely have more balanced beliefs about the uncertainty of the situation and would therefore not find the situation threatening. A visual illustration of the difference between Neil's and Sabrina's reactions to this uncertain situation is depicted in figures 2.1 and 2.2.

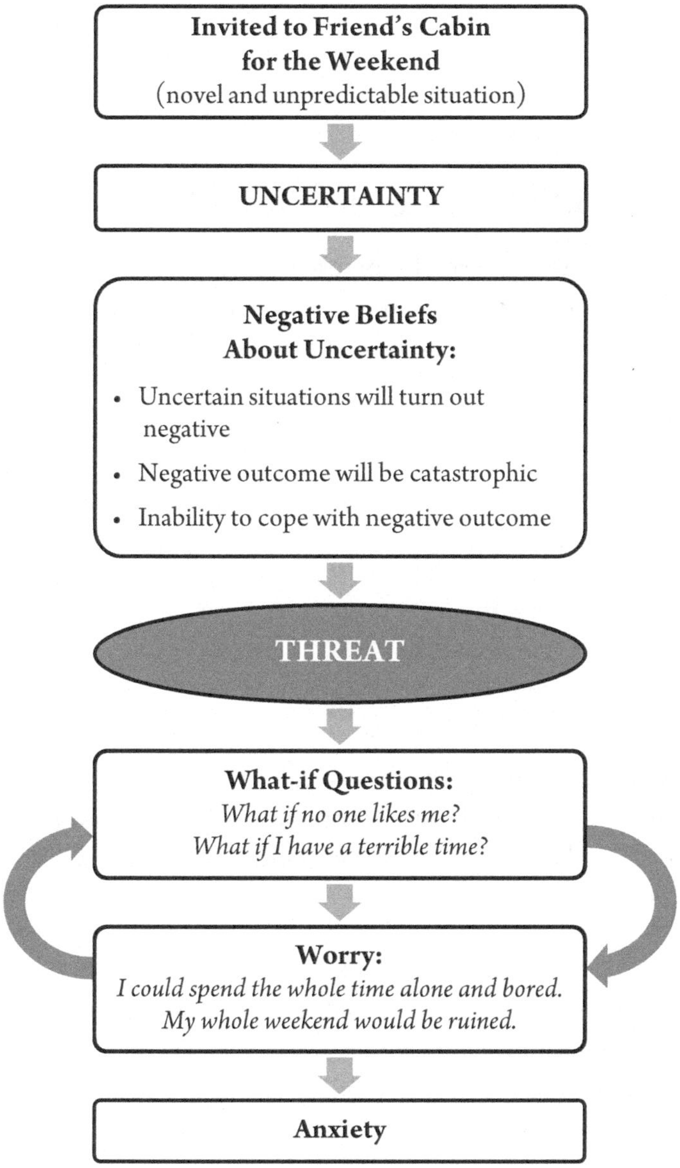

**Invited to Friend's Cabin
for the Weekend**
(novel and unpredictable situation)

⬇

**UNCERTAINTY**

⬇

**Negative Beliefs
About Uncertainty:**

• Uncertain situations will turn out negative

• Negative outcome will be catastrophic

• Inability to cope with negative outcome

⬇

**THREAT**

⬇

**What-if Questions:**
*What if no one likes me?*
*What if I have a terrible time?*

⬇

**Worry:**
*I could spend the whole time alone and bored.
My whole weekend would be ruined.*

⬇

**Anxiety**

Figure 2.1: The impact of Neil's negative
beliefs about uncertainty

---

**Invited to Friend's Cabin
for the Weekend**
(novel and unpredictable
situation)

⬇

**UNCERTAINTY**

⬇

**Balanced Beliefs
About Uncertainty:**

• Uncertain situations will probably turn out all right

• Negative outcomes probably won't be catastrophic

• A negative outcome is likely manageable

⬇

**NO THREAT**

⬇

**End of Cycle**
(no worries)

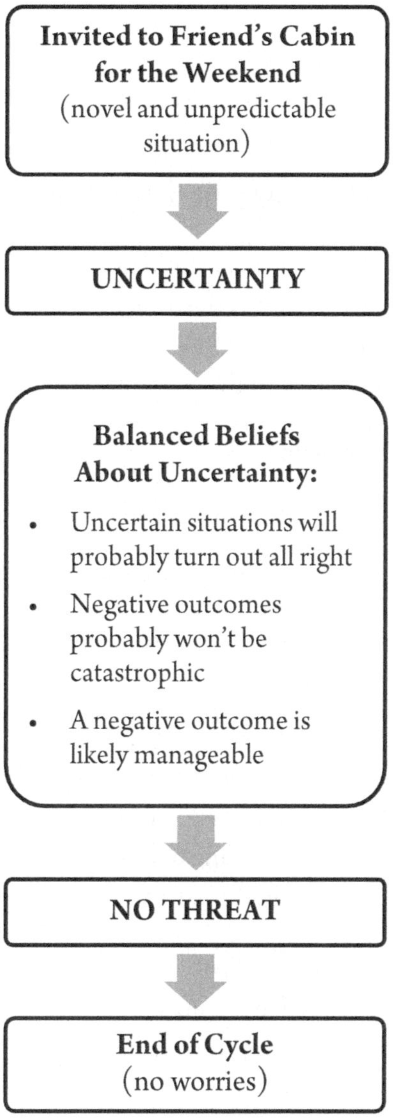

Figure 2.2: The impact of Sabrina's
beliefs about uncertainty

Given that we don't all feel threatened by the same uncertain situations, it's important to recognize not only whether or not you are intolerant of uncertainty, but also what types of uncertain situations are most difficult for you to tolerate. The following exercise is designed to help you identify what kinds of situations trigger your fear and intolerance of uncertainty.

# EXERCISE 2.2:
# What Uncertain Situations Are You Allergic To?

In chapter 1, you identified your most problematic worry topics. In this exercise, you'll review the same topics; however, this time, you'll focus on how much you think you can tolerate the uncertainty in these situations. Read through the examples provided and rate how difficult it is for you to tolerate uncertainty in that area of your life.

**Scoring:**

1 = Not at all difficult to tolerate

2 = Somewhat difficult to tolerate

3 = Very difficult to tolerate

_____ **Health/Physical Symptoms**

Uncertain situations include waiting for the results of medical tests, being unsure why you're experiencing physical symptoms (such as headaches or minor aches and pains), and traveling to different countries where there is a possibility of contracting a disease (such as SARS, Zika virus).

_____ **Danger/Safety**

Uncertain situations include being unsure about the possibility of natural disasters occurring (earthquakes, hurricanes, tsunamis), traveling by car or plane (possibility of a crash occurring), walking alone outside without knowing whether you might be mugged or attacked, and being unsure whether your home could be broken into or could burn down.

_____ **Social Situations**

Uncertain social situations include expressing your opinion to others without knowing how they'll react, talking to new people and being unsure about what to say or whether you'll say something that might offend someone, and being responsible for making plans with friends without being sure you're choosing something others will enjoy.

_____ **Work/School**

Uncertain situations include studying for and taking exams (since you aren't 100 percent sure what will be on the exam) and completing tasks at school or work even though there is the possibility that you might do them incorrectly, make mistakes, or fail to complete them on time.

_____ **Interpersonal Relationships**

These situations include not being absolutely certain about the health of loved ones, about the status of your romantic relationships and friendships (whether your partner will someday leave you or whether a friendship will end), and about the safety and happiness of your children (whether they'll get hurt, struggle in school, or get bullied).

_____ **Daily Activities and Responsibilities**

These situations include leaving the house without being completely sure you locked the door or turned off all the appliances, not being certain throughout the day whether you have your personal items (keys, wallet, phone) with you, going to an appointment with the possibility that you might not get there on time or find parking, and any unexpected changes to your plans or daily routine.

Any other uncertain situations that you find difficult to tolerate?

_____

_____

_____

If you rated a particular life area as being very difficult to tolerate, you probably hold negative beliefs about the uncertainty in those situations.

# Deciding When to Take Risks in Life

When you consider all the potential negative things that could happen in an uncertain situation, it could easily make you think that maybe the best route is simply "Better safe than sorry." It seems to make sense at first that avoiding potential harm might lead to a happier life. However, viewing the uncertainties of life negatively comes at a high price, usually in the form of worry and anxiety, as well as time and energy. For example, someone who's very fearful of uncertainty might spend several hours, days, or weeks researching a decision, such as which day care is best for their children, in an attempt to be certain they're making the right choice. In situations where the outcome matters a great deal, those efforts may be worth it, but in cases where the outcome matters less, it might not be worth the effort.

Let's say you wanted to be certain that you'd find a parking spot close to the theater when going to the movies, so you left an hour early and got a good parking spot as a result. Although you parked close to the theater, you had to leave an hour before the movie even started in order to avoid the minor negative outcome of potentially parking a bit farther away and walking an extra few minutes to the theater. In this example, the effort outweighs the benefits.

Because of this variability in risks versus benefits, it's extremely important to figure out what reasonable risks you're willing to take. If you decide to invite some uncertainty into your life, there is always the possibility that things might go awry. This is true for everyone. It's therefore up to you to decide whether it's worth the risk. In general, viewing uncertainty in a more balanced way makes the world seem less threatening, which results in reduced worry and anxiety—all of which are benefits that seem worth the sacrifice of complete certainty.

# In a Nutshell

In this chapter, you learned about intolerance of uncertainty and how your beliefs about uncertainty impact worry and anxiety. Here are some key points:

- Any situation in which you are not entirely sure of the outcome can be considered an uncertain situation.

- Uncertain situations tend to fall under three categories: (1) novel situations, which involve new or unfamiliar situations you have no prior experience with; (2) ambiguous situations, where the situation itself is not clear or well defined; and (3) unpredictable situations, where you cannot predict the outcome of the situation beforehand.

- Intolerance of uncertainty involves the degree to which you find uncertain situations stressful, negative, and upsetting. The more you are intolerant of uncertainty, the more you're likely to worry, since worry is an attempt to reduce or eliminate uncertainty by mentally planning and preparing for any eventuality.

- People vary greatly in terms of their tolerance for uncertainty. Individuals who are more intolerant of uncertainty tend to hold negative beliefs about uncertainty and its consequences, including the expectation that uncertain situations will have catastrophic outcomes that are beyond the individual's ability to cope. When you have negative beliefs about uncertainty, you're more likely to view uncertain situations as threatening, which in turn leads to worry.

- Individuals who are more tolerant of uncertainty tend to hold balanced beliefs about uncertainty and its consequences. Specifically, a balanced perspective assumes that unless there is evidence to the contrary, uncertain situations will probably turn out all right, and even if they don't, the negative outcome is likely to be manageable and more of a hassle than a horror. When you hold balanced beliefs about uncertainty, you're less likely to view uncertain situations as threatening and, as a result, worry less.

- Not everyone is fearful of the same uncertain situations. You might find that you have negative beliefs about uncertainty in one area of life but that you hold balanced beliefs about uncertainty in another area of life. This explains why people can differ in their reactions to the same situation, with one person potentially becoming worried and anxious and the other not being distressed at all.

Now that you have an understanding of how your beliefs about uncertainty influence your worries, you're in a good position to start tackling your worries at the source. In the next chapter, you'll learn how beliefs about uncertainty not only impact what you think, they also influence what you do.

CHAPTER 3

# Safety Behaviors: Fear of Uncertainty in Action

In the last chapter, you learned how negative beliefs about uncertainty fuel worry. However, fears don't just influence what you *think;* they also influence what you *do.* Whenever you feel threatened, you're likely to cope by taking some action to reduce or avoid the threat. Unfortunately, not all coping behaviors are created equal. Some behaviors can help you deal with your fear in the short term but increase or maintain it over the long term, while other behaviors can help you overcome your fear. But it's not always obvious which actions are most helpful in the long run.

In this chapter, we'll help you recognize whether the actions you take to manage your worries are actually helpful or whether they're unintentionally feeding and maintaining your worries over time.

## Understanding Safety Behaviors

Nobody likes feeling anxious, so it's not surprising that we do things to try to cope. For example, let's say Tony is worried he said something inappropriate in an e-mail to his boss. He might decide to reread it to verify what he wrote, or he might ask his spouse to read the e-mail and reassure him that he didn't write anything inappropriate. Rereading e-mails and asking for reassurance are both deliberate actions Tony is engaging in as an attempt to manage his worries and anxiety. These worry-driven actions are called *safety behaviors.*

Safety behaviors are deliberate actions taken to feel safer in anxiety-provoking situations. When you engage in safety behaviors, you're trying to reduce your anxiety and prevent or minimize a feared outcome (Salkovskis 1991). Let's say you're afraid to fill out a form because you're worried you'll complete it incorrectly. There are many different ways you might cope with this fear. You might have someone else fill it out for you, complete it yourself but review it multiple times, or delay or avoid filling it out. All of these actions are safety behaviors: if you avoid or put off completing the form, you've avoided your feared outcome altogether, and if you either have someone else complete it for you or review your answers multiple times, then you're likely minimizing your feared outcome. Specifically, by procrastinating or avoiding filling out the form, you know you haven't made a mistake because you haven't completed it. If someone else fills it out, then although you aren't entirely sure that it's correct, you know you didn't personally make a mistake. Similarly, if you review it multiple times, your worry that you completed it incorrectly is likely reduced simply because you reviewed your answers. In all cases, your anxiety probably goes down, at least for the moment, because you avoided your feared outcome by engaging in a safety behavior.

## The Problem with Safety Behaviors

At first glance, safety behaviors seem like helpful strategies for coping with anxiety-provoking situations. After all, they can make you feel better by reducing your anxiety, and you don't have to deal with the feared consequences. If, for example, Sharon is worried that she didn't turn off the stove before leaving the house, going back to check seems like a good idea. She won't have to worry all day about a potential fire, and any anxiety she had about the stove being on will disappear once she checks.

So why are safety behaviors problematic? There are two major reasons why safety behaviors are ultimately unhelpful in overcoming your worries. The first is that *anxiety is reduced only in the short term*. That is, you may feel better in the moment, but it'll last only until the next time you're triggered by an uncertain situation and start worrying again. In Sharon's case, she'll feel less anxious once she double-checks that the stove is turned off; however, the next time she leaves the house, she'll be just as anxious and will want to check again. This means that when you use a safety behavior, you have to use that safety behavior every time you're in an anxiety-provoking situation, since your anxiety will return each and every time.

The second reason safety behaviors are unhelpful is that they *actually feed fears over the long term*. As mentioned above, safety behaviors aren't just an attempt at reducing anxiety, they're also designed to help you avoid or minimize a feared outcome. It is this feature of safety behaviors that feeds fears. For example, George is worried about saying something awkward when meeting new people. Consequently, he might decide to only talk to people he knows. By doing so, he successfully avoids the feared outcome of saying or doing something awkward in front of people he doesn't know. In this way, avoidance works!

However, when George engages in the safety behavior of avoiding talking to new people, two other things happen. First, he maintains his belief that his feared outcome would have occurred if he hadn't taken steps to prevent it—that is, he continues to think that he would have said or done something awkward. In other words, whenever you use a safety behavior in an anxiety-provoking situation, you are likely to think that the only reason a particular feared outcome didn't occur is *because* you engaged in the safety behavior.

Second, by avoiding talking to new people, George misses the opportunity to find out whether he is in fact awkward. When he engages in a safety behavior, he becomes unable to find out if his feared outcome would actually have occurred. So one of the biggest problems with safety behaviors is that using them prevents you from finding out whether you even need to use them in the first place.

Given the inherent problems with safety behaviors, they are really only a short-term solution to managing worries. Although they can result in a temporary reduction of anxiety and potentially protect you from feared outcomes, safety behaviors keep your worries and anxiety alive over the long term. For this reason, it's important to recognize your safety behaviors and ultimately learn better strategies for managing your worry and anxiety.

# Identifying Your Own Safety Behaviors

Because people differ with respect to the types of uncertain situations that cause them to worry, there are lots of different safety behaviors people engage in. After reading about safety behaviors, you might have already identified some of the things you do to cope with your worries and anxiety, but there are probably some behaviors you aren't even aware of. The next section will help you identify your safety behaviors.

## *Safety Behaviors and the Fear of Uncertainty*

When it comes to worry, no matter what the topic, safety behaviors are used to reduce or eliminate the uncertainty in a given situation. In general, safety behaviors fall into two categories. The first category is *approach behaviors*. With these types of actions, we're attempting to approach a feared situation and remove as much uncertainty as possible. Let's say you've been experiencing unexplained stomach cramps. To deal with the uncertainty of this situation, you might research your symptoms online, go see your doctor, or discuss your symptoms with others to get reassurance that it's nothing serious. All of these safety behaviors are attempts at removing doubt about the cause and severity of your stomach cramps, by *approaching* the situation and attempting to minimize the uncertainty.

The second category of safety behaviors is called *avoidant behaviors*. These actions are designed to eliminate uncertainty by avoiding the uncertain situation altogether. Let's say you have a job interview and you're worried about not making a good impression. If you engage in avoidant safety behaviors, you might cancel or reschedule the interview. By avoiding or putting off the interview, you have effectively eliminated the uncertainty of making a poor impression. The obvious downside of avoidance behaviors is that you can miss out on opportunities—in this case, a potential new job. You are also usually only delaying the situation until later, when you'll likely have to face it.

# *Safety Behaviors and Worry Themes*

As previously discussed, people can differ with respect to the types of uncertain situations that trigger their negative beliefs about uncertainty. You might be someone who is completely comfortable in social situations but very anxious about uncertainty involving your health. Because of this, you're likely to worry and engage in safety behaviors whenever you experience physical symptoms without a clear cause, but you probably don't worry much when meeting new people.

It can therefore be helpful to focus on identifying the safety behaviors that specifically address your particular worries. Below is a list of major worry themes, along with some common safety behaviors associated with each. You'll probably notice that some safety behaviors appear across several worry themes. This is because the fear of uncertainty and its consequences underlie them all.

**Worries about health/physical symptoms.** If you worry excessively about your health, there are several things you might do to reduce your uncertainty about unknown physical symptoms, including searching medical websites, excessively checking problem areas (like looking at a mole to see if it's grown), making frequent doctor visits, and seeking reassurance from others ("Are you sure you don't think it's something serious?"). Alternatively, you might cope with health worries through avoidance, such as canceling doctor's appointments, not reading articles about health and disease, and deliberately not looking at or touching problem areas.

**Worries about danger/safety.** Most people worry on occasion about safety and natural disasters; however, you might find you worry excessively about these topics. If so, your safety behaviors might include searching online for the frequency of natural disasters, researching the structural integrity of buildings prior to entering them, ensuring you have your survival materials with you (such as an earthquake preparedness kit), frequently repacking or checking survival materials, and avoiding locations where natural disasters have occurred in the past. If you worry frequently about break-ins or being mugged, your safety behaviors might include avoiding walking alone, avoiding going out at night, repeatedly checking door locks (while at home), and leaving lights on in the evening.

**Worries about social situations.** When you interact with other people, you can't be completely sure what they think of you or whether they're enjoying themselves. As such, it's common for people with a fear of uncertainty to worry excessively about social situations, and given that there are many different types of social interactions (meeting new people, being assertive, making small talk), there are lots of associated safety behaviors. If this is one of your worries, you might engage in avoidance safety behaviors by not attending social events, speaking very little if at all, or refraining from giving your opinion. If you use approach safety behaviors, you might plan or rehearse your conversations beforehand to make sure that you don't say something "stupid" and don't run out of things to say.

**Worries about work/school.** Many people worry excessively about their performance at work or school, largely because we have to complete tasks that are graded (at school) or evaluated (at work), and we can't be certain of the outcome. Moreover, our performance can impact our future, with poor grades affecting our ability to get into specific programs or pursue certain careers and poor job performance potentially impacting the likelihood of promotions or keeping a current position.

There are a number of safety behaviors that address the uncertainties of work or school, including excessively checking or reviewing assigned tasks to ensure they're completed correctly, seeking reassurance from others about your performance, and procrastinating or avoiding tasks when you aren't sure that you can complete them correctly. In addition, you might refuse to delegate tasks to colleagues, since you can't be certain they'll complete them to your standards, or you might always delegate unfamiliar tasks to others to avoid making mistakes yourself.

**Worries about interpersonal relationships.** If you worry excessively about loved ones, your safety behaviors might include frequent check-ins, like repeatedly texting your child or spouse when they're out to make sure they're okay. Some people worry about friendships or romantic relationships because they're not 100 percent sure they'll last, and they cope with this by deliberately avoiding starting relationships or only partially committing to friendships or romantic relationships. Alternatively, some people seek out excessive reassurance from friends and romantic partners about how the relationship is going.

**Worries about daily activities and responsibilities.** If you worry about completing daily tasks or chores correctly (such as locking doors, doing the laundry, or filling out paperwork), your safety behaviors might include doing certain tasks yourself (not allowing other family members to do laundry in order to be completely certain that it's done correctly), repeatedly rechecking things, or asking others to check that you completed tasks properly. You might also engage in avoidant safety behaviors by putting off or avoiding tasks by asking others to do them for you.

Some people worry about minor things that arise throughout the day, such as unexpected changes to their routine, getting somewhere on time, getting lost, finding a parking spot, remembering to do things, or losing something. Associated safety behaviors might include keeping a very predictable routine, excessively planning your day, keeping detailed to-do lists, leaving way ahead of time for work or appointments, pre-planning your route to new destinations, or constantly checking to make sure you have your phone, wallet, or keys.

Now that you're familiar with some of the common safety behaviors associated with different worry themes, the next exercise can help you begin to identify your specific safety behaviors.

# EXERCISE 3.1:
## Identifying Your Safety Behaviors

Because you might not notice some of the things you do to reduce or avoid uncertainty, it can be helpful to spend some time monitoring your worries and subsequent safety behaviors. The following form can help you track and record this. In order to get a good picture of the different types of safety behaviors you use in various situations, we recommend completing the form up to three times a day for at least a week.

When completing this worksheet, use your anxiety as a cue to observe what's going on: write down the situation you're in (trigger), your worries about it (worry), and what you did (or would like to do) to cope with the situation (safety behavior). It's a good idea to complete this worksheet as soon as possible while your memories are fresh. Although we've discussed how safety behaviors are ultimately unhelpful in overcoming your worries in the long term, don't forget that you haven't learned any alternative strategies yet. As such, when you recognize a safety behavior, this doesn't mean you need to stop doing it. The goal at this point is solely to recognize your safety behaviors, not change them.

To help you to complete this worksheet, some examples of worries and associated safety behaviors are shown below. (A PDF of the blank worksheet for your use is available at http://www.newharbinger.com/40064.)

| Date/Time | Trigger | Worry (what-if question) | Anxiety (0 to 10) | Safety Behavior (what you did) |
|---|---|---|---|---|
| Sunday 10 a.m. | Working on completing an essay for school | What if it's not perfect? I might get a failing grade. | 6 | Rewrote the essay several times. Asked my parents to read it and reassure me that it was perfect. |
| Friday 9 p.m. | My son is late coming home | What if he got into an accident? He might be in trouble and need help. | 9 | Texted my son repeatedly. Called his friends to ask if they knew where he was. Called the police to see if any accident had been reported recently. |

| Date/Time | Trigger | Worry (what-if question) | Anxiety (0 to 10) | Safety Behavior (what you did) |
|---|---|---|---|---|
| | | | | |
| | | | | |
| | | | | |
| | | | | |
| | | | | |
| | | | | |
| | | | | |
| | | | | |

Completing this worksheet for at least a week will give you an idea of your typical safety behaviors. If you're having difficulty identifying them, complete it for several weeks. The information you obtain will be used in later chapters to help you tackle your worries, so take as much time as needed to get an accurate picture of your safety behaviors.

## *Aren't Some Safety Behaviors Helpful?*

Many of the safety behaviors that we identified as problematic are actions that most people engage in from time to time. For example, it's common for people to make to-do lists, reread an e-mail or text before sending, or ask someone for advice before making a decision. In fact, some of the behaviors that we identified as safety behaviors might even seem like useful actions. To make sure you completed a task correctly, it makes sense to double-check or review your work. As such, you might be wondering whether some of these behaviors are normal and appropriate. It's true that some safety behaviors can be helpful strategies in day-to-day life. However, it's not really *what* you do that determines whether an action is a safety behavior, but rather *why* and *how often* you do it.

Let's say that you ride your bicycle or walk everywhere. This can be a very healthy lifestyle choice *depending on why you do it.* If you're biking and walking everywhere because you think it's good exercise, then these actions are likely based on choice, not fear. That is, you prefer to bike or walk because it seems like a healthy decision; however, if you had to take a vehicle to get somewhere, you would. If, on the other hand, you're biking and walking in order to avoid being stuck in a vehicle in case you have a panic attack, the reasons behind your actions are very different. In this case, traveling by bike or on foot is actually an avoidant safety behavior designed to protect you from the uncertainty of potentially having a panic attack in a confined space. In other words, biking or walking everywhere is an action taken out of fear.

The other way to determine if an action is a safety behavior lies in the frequency of the action: *how often* you do it. As mentioned above, making to-do lists, rereading e-mails, and even double-checking door locks are all appropriate actions provided that you're only doing them *on occasion.* If, however, you can't ever go to the grocery store without a list, spend a great deal of time rereading every single e-mail and text, or repeatedly check to make sure your front door is locked, then these actions are probably safety behaviors. Not only are these behaviors time-consuming, but the fact that you're doing them frequently suggests they're driven by anxiety.

When your behaviors are dictated by worry and anxiety, it's worth targeting them for change. Once you've overcome your worries in a particular situation, you can then decide to return to the same behavior if you want to. For example, after you overcome the fear of having a panic attack in an enclosed space, you might decide that although you're no longer afraid of being in a car, you still prefer to get around by bike or on foot for health reasons. However, you'll have the added benefit of knowing you're doing what you want to do, not what anxiety will allow you to do.

## *Catching Your Safety Behaviors*

Despite tracking your safety behaviors, you still might find it challenging to identify what you do. This is because the fear of uncertainty is the fear of a characteristic of a situation, as opposed to the situation itself. If you're afraid of dogs, it's relatively easy to identify what you do to cope with that fear, since you can observe your actions when you see a dog. But it can be tricky to observe your actions when you fear the uncertainty in a situation.

First, the fear of uncertainty is an abstract fear, unlike the concrete fear of a dog: you can see a dog, but you can't see uncertainty. Second, it's not always obvious that your worry is due to the uncertainty in a given situation. Because of this, it's important to be patient and give yourself time to recognize how the fear of uncertainty influences your thoughts and actions. Learning to recognize your uncertainty-driven safety behaviors is an acquired skill that you'll work on throughout this workbook.

The next exercise is designed to further assist you in recognizing your typical safety behaviors.

# EXERCISE 3.2:
# Recognizing Uncertainty-Driven Safety Behaviors

Read through the list of common safety behaviors below and place a check next to every type you have used. In addition, write down personal examples of times when you used that specific safety behavior.

Remember that an action is only a safety behavior if it's driven by anxiety or you do it frequently in order to reduce or avoid uncertainty. It's the motivation behind an action, rather than the action itself, that will tell you whether a behavior is problematic. You might find it helpful to use your worksheet from exercise 3.1 to complete this exercise.

## Common Uncertainty-Driven Safety Behaviors

_____    **Avoidance**

This can involve avoiding any situation or activity that is novel, ambiguous, or unpredictable, including avoiding making decisions, not sharing your thoughts or opinions, or always agreeing with others in social situations to avoid the uncertainty of potentially displeasing them.

*Personal examples:* _____

_____

_____

_____ **Procrastination**

This involves deliberately putting off or delaying completing tasks or making decisions in novel, ambiguous, or unpredictable situations.

_Personal examples:_ _____

_____

_____

_____ **Impulsive Decision Making**

This involves dealing with decision making (and the uncertainty of making the wrong decision) by either making a random choice (such as by coin toss) or deliberately waiting until the last minute before deciding, to reduce responsibility for the choice.

_Personal examples:_ _____

_____

_____

_____ **Partial Commitment**

This involves failing to fully commit to relationships, activities, or decisions because you're not certain of the outcome.

_Personal examples:_ _____

_____

_____

_____ **Transferring Responsibility to Others**

This involves asking others to complete tasks or make decisions in order to avoid the uncertainty of making a mistake or making the wrong choice.

_Personal examples:_ _____

_____

_____

_____ **Doing Everything Yourself**

This involves never delegating tasks to others so you can be sure that things are completed to your standards.

_Personal examples:_ _____

_____

_____

_____ **Excessive Reassurance Seeking**

This involves asking others repeatedly for advice when making a decision, for reassurances that a task or activity was completed correctly, and for confirmation that things are safe. Reassurance seeking is an attempt to minimize uncertainty by trying to obtain consensus from others that everything is okay or that a decision was correct.

_Personal examples:_ _____

_____

_____

_____ **Checking**

This involves repeatedly reviewing completed tasks or actions to make sure they were completed correctly. This can include rereading or rewriting completed written materials (e-mails, texts, essays, or work reports) or rechecking locks or household appliances.

*Personal examples:* _____

_____

_____

_____ **Excessive Information Seeking**

This involves obtaining an overabundance of information, either online or by going to multiple sources (for example, stores, doctors) to be certain that you have all the information you need when making a decision or when unsure about a situation (like medical conditions).

*Personal examples:* _____

_____

_____

_____ **Excessive Preparation**

This can include spending an extraordinary amount of time planning and preparing for activities (for example, planning a dinner party, packing for a trip), making multiple or extensive to-do lists to ensure that you don't forget anything, and planning or rehearsing conversations ahead of time to be sure that there's always something to discuss.

*Personal examples:* _____

_____

_____

Hopefully, going through this list has helped you recognize your safety behaviors, especially those you may not have realized you engage in. You'll be using this information to complete exercises in the next chapter.

# In a Nutshell

In this chapter, you learned about safety behaviors and how they may fuel worry and anxiety. Here are some key points:

- Safety behaviors involve any deliberate action you take to cope with an anxiety-provoking situation. Safety behaviors are used to reduce anxiety in the moment and to avoid or minimize a feared outcome.

- Safety behaviors are problematic for two reasons. First, although they reduce anxiety in the moment, they maintain anxiety and fear in the long term. Second, safety behaviors prevent us from finding out whether a feared outcome would actually occur if a safety behavior wasn't used. Safety behaviors might make us feel better in the moment, but they keep fears alive in the long run.

- With respect to worry, safety behaviors fall into two categories: (1) approach behaviors, which are actions designed to reduce or eliminate the uncertainty in a given situation; and (2) avoidant behaviors, which are actions designed to cope with uncertainty by avoiding an uncertain situation altogether.

- Safety behaviors are not inherently negative. It's not what you do in response to worry that is the problem; it's why and how often you do it. When you're deliberately doing something to avoid or reduce uncertainty, then you're not *choosing* to do it—you're actually compelled to do it out of fear.

Now that you have a good understanding of worry, safety behaviors, and how the fear of uncertainty fuels these thoughts and actions, we can turn our attention to the strategies that will help you break the worry cycle by throwing a wrench into the engine of worry.

# CHAPTER 4

# Is Uncertainty Dangerous? Testing It Out

By now you know that it's our beliefs about uncertainty that fuel the engine of worry: If we have nega-tive beliefs about uncertainty, we're more fearful and intolerant of uncertainty, and as a result, we worry excessively when faced with uncertain situations. If, on the other hand, we hold balanced beliefs about uncertainty, we're less likely to be threatened by uncertain events, and therefore we worry less.

This means that the best way to reduce your worries is not to tackle the worries themselves, but instead to directly target your beliefs about uncertainty. This has the benefit of targeting what under-lies worry in the first place, rather than trying to manage each individual worry (a strategy that is time-consuming and often only minimally effective). This also means that changing your beliefs about the threat of uncertainty will help you reduce your worries no matter what you worry about.

But how do you change a belief? It's easy to say that it's a good idea to think differently about uncertain situations. It's entirely different to actually *believe* that uncertain situations might not be as threatening as we think. In this chapter, we'll explore how you can change your beliefs, and we'll provide concrete strategies to help you think differently about the threat of uncertainty.

## Testing Out the Dangers of Uncertainty

Changing our beliefs about anything can be difficult. It's not a matter of simply trying to "think posi-tive." If you've ever tried this when feeling anxious, you probably found that it wasn't very successful. This is because when we believe something, we aren't just being pessimistic or obstinate: we believe what we believe because *we think it's true.* When you're faced with an uncertain situation, you likely believe, at least in the moment, that the situation is in fact threatening and requires intervention on your part. Simply telling yourself that it'll probably be fine won't work. The challenge is therefore to change your belief about what you *think* is true. The best way to do this is by figuring out whether a given belief is *actually* true.

# Learning to Change Your Mind

It can seem overwhelming to consider changing your entire perspective on uncertain situations and the threat they might present. However, we've all changed our minds at various times, on topics as wide-ranging as political and social issues to our favorite television show. In general, we change our beliefs about something when there's compelling evidence to do so. Let's say you want to convince a friend to ride his bicycle to work instead of driving his car. How would you go about doing this? You'd probably present arguments in favor of riding a bike and against driving a car. For example, you might discuss the health benefits of riding a bike, the positive impact on the environment, how fun biking is, and the minimal increase in time it would take to get to work. You might also mention the frustration of being caught in traffic and the cost of gas and parking. If your case is compelling, your friend might change his mind, provided he believes the arguments that riding a bike to work would be better overall for him.

This same logic can be applied to negative beliefs about uncertainty. As we saw in chapter 2, worry makes sense if you believe that uncertain situations will be catastrophically bad and that you'll be unable to cope with negative outcomes. This belief may not be accurate, but in order to potentially change it, we would need a compelling case in favor of balanced beliefs about uncertainty. If you're able to compile evidence that disproves the accuracy of your negative beliefs about uncertainty and instead suggests that uncertain situations are not as threatening as you thought, then you will probably change your beliefs. So how do you gather this evidence?

# Targeting Safety Behaviors

One of the biggest roadblocks to obtaining evidence against the threat of uncertainty is the use of safety behaviors. We engage in safety behaviors to reduce anxiety and prevent negative outcomes in feared situations. However, safety behaviors paradoxically keep fears alive by preventing us from finding out whether a negative outcome would have occurred. We collect no evidence one way or the other, and all we have to go on is our original belief that there would likely have been a negative outcome if we hadn't intervened through the use of safety behaviors. The problem is not that we are incorrect: it's possible that a negative outcome could occur without the use of a safety behavior. The problem is that we don't know. Our safety behaviors prevent us from ever discovering whether our negative beliefs about uncertainty are accurate.

Let's say Gina has an appointment with her doctor. She might worry, *What if I'm late getting to the doctor's office and can't find parking? The doctor could be so angry with me for being late that he refuses to see me and won't let me make another appointment! I won't be able to find another family doctor willing to see me!* Because of these worries, Gina decides to leave early and take a taxi rather than try to find a parking spot. Using these safety behaviors, she arrives early for her appointment, thus avoiding all her feared expectations. However, Gina doesn't know whether she would have been late if she left at a reasonable time, if she would have had difficulty finding parking, or if her doctor would have been upset by her lateness. Without this information, she maintains her negative beliefs and may continue to worry about arriving on time for things, therefore continuing to leave early and avoiding driving her car so she doesn't have to look for parking. In other words, Gina has no opportunity to test her feared predictions and thereby gather evidence that might challenge her negative beliefs.

## Testing Out Negative Beliefs

As discussed in chapter 2, there are three main negative beliefs we can have about uncertainty, and it's these beliefs that need to be tested in order to reduce worry: (1) uncertain situations will turn out negative; (2) negative outcomes will be catastrophic; and (3) you'll be unable to cope with negative outcomes. Gina's worries reflect all of these beliefs. Since she's not 100 percent sure how long it will take her to get to the doctor's office, she's worried that she'll be late and not find parking (negative outcome), that the doctor will be upset about her lateness and refuse to give her another appointment (catastrophic outcome), and that she won't be able to find another family doctor as a result (inability to cope with negative outcomes).

Because Gina used the safety behaviors of leaving early and taking a taxi, she's unable to determine whether her feared predictions would have occurred. The best way for her to test out these predictions and the accuracy of her beliefs is to deliberately refrain from using her safety behaviors in order to observe what the actual outcome in this situation would be. Testing your beliefs in this manner is called a *behavioral experiment*.

# Conducting Behavioral Experiments

Behavioral experiments are a therapeutic strategy used in cognitive behavioral therapy. They allow for direct testing of the accuracy of our beliefs by deliberately entering a feared situation, making a prediction about what we expect will occur, and then observing and recording the actual outcome. In this way, we can objectively determine whether feared expectations do in fact occur. In the rest of this chapter, you'll learn how to construct behavioral experiments, tailoring them to your own particular safety behaviors and worries, and how to use them to gather evidence about the accuracy of those worries.

## Constructing a Behavioral Experiment

Before you can conduct a behavioral experiment, you need to construct an effective one. As a first step, you'll need to identify a situation for which you have a specific prediction about what you fear will occur, as well as a safety behavior you typically use to prevent that feared outcome from occurring.

When engaging in a behavioral experiment, you have the opportunity to directly test your prediction by not engaging in the safety behavior.

In Gina's case, a good first experiment would be to drive herself to an appointment and not leave early. Her prediction for this experiment might be: *I'll be late to meet my friend because I'll have a hard time finding parking, and my friend will be angry with me. We'll lose our reservation, and our lunch date will be ruined.* As you can see, she has identified her feared outcomes in advance (lateness, difficulty parking, angry friend) so that she can later compare those feared outcomes to what actually happened.

When Gina conducts this exercise, she'll be able to assess the accuracy of her negative beliefs about uncertainty by determining whether her feared outcomes are a correct reflection of the actual outcome. It's possible that when Gina conducts her experiment, the actual outcome is generally positive: she arrives on time, quickly finds parking, and her lunch date goes well. In this case, the results of this experiment have provided her with some preliminary evidence against her feared outcomes. Gina is now able to use these findings to directly test the accuracy of her negative beliefs about uncertainty by framing her feared outcomes as questions:

1. Did the uncertain situation turn out negative? *Not in this case. I arrived on time, and my lunch date went well.*

2. If the outcome was negative, how bad was it? *There was no negative outcome.*

3. If the outcome was negative, how did you handle it? *No coping was needed, because the outcome was positive.*

Because the actual outcome of Gina's experiment was generally positive, she was only able to test the accuracy of the first negative belief about uncertainty (uncertain events will have a negative outcome)—the remaining two beliefs did not apply. But let's say Gina's experiment had a negative outcome: she *did* arrive late because there was traffic and she *did* have trouble finding parking. Using these findings, Gina now has the opportunity to evaluate the accuracy of all three negative beliefs about uncertainty:

1. Did the uncertain situation turn out negative? *Yes. There was traffic, and I didn't find parking right away, so I ended up being fifteen minutes late.*

2. If the outcome was negative, how bad was it? *It wasn't good to be late, but it wasn't as bad as I expected. My friend was not upset, and there was no problem with the reservation.*

3. If the outcome was negative, how did you handle it? *When I realized I was running late, I texted my friend to let her know. She said it wasn't a problem, and she let the restaurant host know I was on my way.*

So, in this case, Gina was able to discover that even when the outcome was negative (she was late), it was not catastrophic. Moreover, she found out that she was in fact able to cope with the situation effectively.

This type of behavioral experiment is a good first step toward gathering evidence about what actually occurs in uncertain situations. And as you might guess, it's important to run these sorts of experiments multiple times to gather a sizable body of evidence. If the evidence consistently shows that uncertain situations often turn out all right and that even when outcomes are negative, they're manageable and not catastrophic, then over time you're likely to change the way you think about the threat of uncertainty.

Now that you know how behavioral experiments are conducted, it's time to begin developing your own in the next exercise.

# EXERCISE 4.1:
## Identifying Your Own Behavioral Experiments

Because not everyone worries about the same topics, the types of behavioral experiments that are most helpful will differ according to the person. To identify those that will be most helpful to you, review the list of experiments categorized by worry type below and write down for each one the level of anxiety you would expect it to elicit from 0 (no anxiety at all) to 10 (overwhelming anxiety). Some experiments have variations written in parentheses; these are designed to potentially alter the anxiety of the situation (for example, increasing the amount of time engaged in the experiment). If the situation in question is anxiety-provoking for you, record the anxiety level you'd expect for each variation.

There is also space for you to write down some of your own ideas for experiments. You can use the information you obtained about your safety behaviors in exercises 3.1 and 3.2 to help you come up with behavioral experiments. When doing so, remember that behavioral experiments should involve deliberately facing an uncertain situation without using a safety behavior to reduce or avoid that uncertainty.

### Experiments Targeting Health/Physical Symptoms

_____ When experiencing a mild physical sensation without a clear cause (headache, muscle pain), do not look up the symptom online, seek reassurance from family or friends, or visit the doctor for 24 hours (or 48 hours _____ or 72 hours _____)

If you are someone who avoids doctor visits or reading articles about health and disease:

_____ Make a doctor's appointment for a checkup

_____ Go for a checkup at the doctor's office

_____ Watch or read articles or segments on health issues (for example, cancer, Alzheimer's) without seeking reassurance from family or friends

What other experiments targeting health/physical symptoms can you think of?

_____

_____

## Experiments Targeting Danger/Safety

_____ Go for a walk by yourself on a downtown (or residential _____) street during the day (or evening _____)

_____ Turn off all the lights while in your home at night (other than the light in the room you are in)

_____ Turn off all the lights in your home when going to bed

_____ Visit a large building alone (or with family members _____) without looking up its structural integrity

_____ Avoid checking your earthquake preparedness kit or survival materials for at least a week (or two weeks _____ or one month _____)

_____ Take a vacation to a new city (or a new country _____) without researching the frequency of natural disasters in the area

What other experiments targeting danger/safety can you think of?

_____

_____

## Experiments Targeting Social Situations

_____ Give your opinion about a movie or restaurant to a friend (or a group of friends _____) without waiting for everyone else's opinion first

_____ Give a different opinion about a movie or restaurant than a friend (or a group a friends)

_____ Share your ideas or opinions on work- or school-related topics to coworkers, supervisors, or fellow students

_____ Politely decline an invitation (for example, going to lunch with colleagues) without providing excessive apologies or excuses

_____ Accept an invitation to a party or social gathering (and actually attend _____)

_____ While at a social gathering, make eye contact or engage in conversation with someone you don't know that well (or someone you don't know at all _____)

_____ Have a brief conversation with an acquaintance or colleague without rehearsing or preparing the conversation beforehand

_____ Sign up and go to a class (for example, an exercise class) by yourself (or with a friend _____)

What other experiments targeting social situations can you think of?

_____

_____

## Experiments Targeting Work/School

_____ Check your work or school assignment only once (or not at all _____) before handing it in

_____ Hand in work or school assignments without seeking reassurance from others

_____ Complete a work or school assignment prior to the deadline (that is, do not procrastinate) and then hand it in

_____ Delegate a task to a colleague; depending on what is most anxiety-provoking for you, you can either check in on your colleague's progress (but refrain from giving advice or suggestions) or don't check in on their progress at all

_____ Hand in a school assignment and then don't check with the professor to ensure that it was received

_____ Accept an unfamiliar task at work (that you would normally delegate) and refrain from seeking reassurance or information (or ask only once for necessary information _____)

What other experiments targeting work/school can you think of?

_____

_____

## Experiments Targeting Interpersonal Relationships

_____ Do not check your cell phone for e-mails, texts, or phone calls for at least one hour (or two hours _____ or three hours _____)

_____ Phone or text family members (spouse, parents, children) only once (or twice _____ or not at all _____) during an entire day

_____ Do not phone or text your family members if they are less than 10 minutes late (or 15 minutes _____ or 30 minutes _____) coming home

_____ Allow your partner (or a friend) to make plans for an outing without telling you ahead of time what you will be doing

_____ Make plans for you and your partner (or a friend) without telling the other person ahead of time what you will be doing

_____ Contact a friend you haven't spoken to in a while (without planning the conversation)

_____ Accept a spontaneous invitation from a friend or family member to a social activity

_____ Make firm plans with a friend or family member at least one week (or two weeks _____) in advance (and do not cancel at the last minute)

What other experiments targeting interpersonal relationships can you think of?

_____

_____

## Experiments Targeting Daily Activities and Responsibilities

_____ Delegate a household chore to a family member without telling them how to do it or watching over them while they do it

_____ Make a minor change in your daily routine (for example, go somewhere or try something new for lunch, change the time you go to the gym, have your spouse pick up the kids)

_____ Don't leave early for an appointment (and don't call ahead to explain that you might be late)

_____ Go to the grocery store without a list

_____ Refrain from making a to-do list for one day (or two days _____ or one week _____)

_____ Try a new restaurant or go see a movie without reading reviews first

_____ Make a minor decision (where to eat lunch, what to wear to work) without seeking reassurance or information online

_____ Make a minor purchase (new clothing) without asking for the opinion of others

_____ Take on a household chore that you usually delegate to others (doing the laundry, making dinner)

_____ Leave the house without checking to ensure that your appliances are turned off (or check only once _____)

What other experiments targeting daily activities and responsibilities can you think of?

_____

_____

In the next sections, you'll use the information you obtained from this exercise to help you develop your own behavioral experiments.

# *Tips for Developing Useful Behavioral Experiments*

Although behavioral experiments are one of the most powerful strategies for challenging negative thoughts, it's important to develop and complete experiments the optimal way. Here are some tips to ensure that your behavioral experiments are as successful and helpful as possible.

**Chase anxiety.** When you're completing a behavioral experiment, you're deliberately facing your feared predictions about uncertain situations. As a result, you can expect to feel anxious. In fact, not only should you anticipate anxiety, but you should also be "chasing" it to make sure you're on the right track. If you're not anxious when completing an experiment, you may have inadvertently replaced one safety behavior with another. For example, let's say Daniel's experiment was to leave his home without checking the stove. If he wasn't anxious when leaving his home, it might be because he replaced the safety behavior of checking with other behaviors, such as deliberately not using the stove or having his partner check the stove instead.

**Start small.** Because facing your fears through behavioral experiments is anxiety-provoking, it's best to start small. Initial experiments should cause only mild to moderate anxiety (a score of 3 or 4 on a scale of 1 to 10). If you try to complete experiments that are too difficult in the beginning and you are unable to follow through on them, you are more likely to get discouraged and give up trying. The most important part of behavioral experiments is actually doing them, so it doesn't matter how small your first experiments are: where you start is not where you will finish.

**Keep the stakes low at first.** Because you're deliberately inviting uncertainty into your life when conducting a behavioral experiment, there's always the possibility that an experiment could yield a negative outcome (for example, Daniel could leave the stove on). This is one of the reasons why behavioral experiments are challenging. To keep your initial experiments small, it's a good idea to first conduct experiments in which the stakes are low, so your anxiety remains manageable. In Gina's example, not leaving early to meet a friend was a good first experiment, since although it would be anxiety-provoking to be late for her lunch date with her friend, it would be less difficult than not leaving early (and potentially being late) for an important meeting with her boss. As your confidence grows after engaging in more experiments, you can choose higher-stakes behavioral experiments.

**Complete multiple experiments.** To think differently about the threat of a situation, you need lots of evidence against your beliefs. Having one positive (or one negative) outcome in a behavioral experiment can be an interesting finding, but it's unlikely to change the way you think. For example, in Gina's experiment, if she'd arrived on time to meet her friend for lunch, she would probably think she'd been lucky but would retain her belief that the next time she didn't leave early for an appointment, she'd be late. If she conducted this behavioral experiment several times, though, across different types of appointments, and if she either arrived on schedule every time or was able to manage any lateness quite easily, then she would probably begin to think differently about both the need to always leave early and the threat of that particular uncertain situation. It is therefore a good idea to repeat behavioral experiments when you can, to accumulate lots of evidence.

**Record your findings.** Writing down your findings from behavioral experiments serves several purposes. First, you'll be able to directly contrast your feared outcomes to your actual outcomes, because you recorded them. This is more powerful than just remembering what happened. Second, recording your findings allows you to build a powerful case against the accuracy of your negative beliefs about uncertainty. You'll be able to review all your findings and make conclusions about what generally occurs when you face uncertain situations and how you react overall to negative outcomes when they arise. Finally, by recording your findings, you will be able to directly observe your progress. Over time, you might be surprised to see your experiments becoming gradually more challenging, and experiments that were initially difficult becoming easier to complete. Given the time and effort it takes to work through the strategies in this workbook and manage your worries and anxiety, a record of your successes and achievements is a good thing to have.

# EXERCISE 4.2:
## Starting Your Behavioral Experiments

This exercise involves setting up and completing your own behavioral experiments. Use the list of potential behavioral experiments from exercise 4.1 to identify the experiments you expect to cause you mild to moderate anxiety (scores of 3 or 4). We recommend that you complete two or three experiments a week, so try to identify at least a couple that you'd be willing to try for the first week.

Write down the experiments you are willing to try this week:

1. _____

2. _____

3. _____

For each experiment, use the blank worksheet provided (also available at http://www.newharbinger .com/40064). *Prior to conducting* your experiment, write down what you will be doing (experiment) and what you are worried will happen (feared outcome). *After you complete your experiment,* write down what actually happened (actual outcome) and, if the outcome was negative, how you handled the situation in the moment (coping). Here's an example of a completed behavioral experiment worksheet:

| Experiment (what you will be doing) | Feared Outcome (what you are worried will happen) | Actual Outcome (what actually happened) | Coping (if the outcome was negative, how you handled it) |
|---|---|---|---|
| Let my child pack her own soccer bag (delegated task) | She'll forget to pack some equipment, and she won't be able to play; coach will be mad, she'll be upset. | She forgot to pack her knee pads; she asked her coach for a spare pair and used those instead. | No coping necessary; daughter handled it herself |
| Make plans for me and my partner without asking for reassurance | He won't like the activity I picked; he'll be upset. We will have a terrible time; evening will be ruined. | We had a great time. My partner was really happy with my choice. | No coping necessary |
| Buy a new lens for my camera without researching online | I'll get the wrong lens. I'll be upset and will have wasted lots of time and effort. | I realized that I did buy the wrong lens when I got home. | Went back to store and exchanged it for the right lens (took about 30 minutes) |

Things to keep in mind for your first experiments:

- *Plan your experiments* before doing them. You want to think about what you're going to do and what you're worried will happen *before* you do the experiment. We sometimes get thrown into uncertain situations against our wishes (like a friend changing social plans at the last minute), but it's not a behavioral experiment unless you *choose* to deliberately enter into an uncertain situation.

- Make sure that your behavioral experiment has an *observable outcome*. You should be able to observe and record what actually happened shortly after the experiment. For example, if you don't check your cell phone for an hour, after the hour has passed, you will be able to observe right away what happened (no one called, you missed a text).

- You can *repeat the same experiment* multiple times (such as not checking your cell phone for a predetermined amount of time) in a given week or, if you prefer, you can *try different experiments* each week.

| Experiment (what you will be doing) | Feared Outcome (what you are worried will happen) | Actual Outcome (what actually happened) | Coping (if the outcome was negative, how you handled it) |
|---|---|---|---|
|  |  |  |  |
|  |  |  |  |
|  |  |  |  |
|  |  |  |  |
|  |  |  |  |
|  |  |  |  |

At the end of each week, take stock of your experiments to see what information you uncovered about the accuracy of your negative beliefs about uncertainty. The next exercise will help you review the findings from your weekly behavioral experiments.

It's a good idea to reflect on behavioral experiments and evaluate what the findings tell you about the outcomes of uncertain situations and your ability to handle negative outcomes should they occur. To do this, it can be helpful to ask yourself some questions about your weekly experiments, which can provide you with an overall view of the results. Key questions and sample answers based on the examples are presented here:

1.  How often was the actual outcome positive or neutral? *One of the three outcomes was positive. My partner and I had a great evening when I picked the activity without asking for reassurance.*

2.  How often was the actual outcome negative? *Two of the three experiments had a negative outcome: when I let my daughter pack her own soccer bag, she forgot her knee pads, and when I purchased a new lens for my camera without researching it first, I actually bought the wrong lens.*

3.  When (and if) the outcomes were negative, were they as bad as expected? *Neither was very bad. Actually, I think it was good for my daughter to learn how to pack her own soccer bag and figure out how to deal with forgetting things on her own. It was inconvenient to go back to the store to pick up the correct lens for my camera, but it didn't take much time to sort out and I wasn't as upset about it as I thought I would be.*

4.  When (and if) the outcomes were negative, how do you think you handled the situation? *The only situation I really dealt with was getting the wrong camera lens. It was a hassle to go back to the store, but it was easy to fix. I think I handled it very well. My daughter handled the situation of the forgotten knee pads on her own by talking to her coach. It was probably a good experience for her to sort out this kind of problem on her own.*

5.  So far, what are the results of the behavioral experiments telling you about the outcomes of uncertain situations and your ability to handle them? *So far, things have turned out better than expected. I had a good time with my partner when I planned the evening without getting reassurance. The other two experiments had negative outcomes, but they were quite minor. I got the opportunity to see that I could handle a situation quite well (I went back to the store to get the right camera lens), and my daughter also got the opportunity to sort out a problem on her own. It seems, at least right now, that when uncertain events do have negative outcomes, they really aren't that bad and I'm capable of handling them.*

In the next exercise, you can answer these questions using the findings from your own experiments.

## EXERCISE 4.3:
# Summarizing the Findings from Your Behavioral Experiments

Answer the following questions at the end of each week about the experiments you undertook that week (this questionnaire is also available as a PDF at http://www.newharbinger.com/40064). When you answer the fifth and final question, do so with *all* of the behavioral experiments you have completed since you started in mind.

1. How often was the actual outcome positive or neutral? _____

_____

_____

2. How often was the actual outcome negative? _____

_____

_____

3. When (and if) the outcomes were negative, were they as bad as expected? _____

_____

_____

4. When (and if) the outcomes were negative, how do you think you handled the situation?

_____

_____

5.   So far, what are the results of the behavioral experiments telling you about the outcomes of uncertain situations and your ability to handle them?

_____

_____

_____

Because we don't truly change our minds about anything unless there is compelling evidence that can't be accounted for simply by luck or chance, it is recommended that you complete two to three behavioral experiments a week for at least a month. At the end of each week, don't forget to review your overall findings.

## Troubleshooting Your Experiments

It can be challenging to set up your own behavioral experiments. Here are some common difficulties you might face, along with how to handle them.

### Can't Get Started Completing Experiments

Because behavioral experiments lead to feelings of anxiety, it's completely normal to be reluctant to start trying them out. After all, you're anticipating a negative outcome when you deliberately invite uncertainty into your life. However, if you've decided that you want to address your worries head-on, behavioral experiments are the way to do it.

A good way to get started is to plan your first experiments as concretely as possible: pick the day and time that you will be completing them and note it in your agenda, if possible. Write down the experiments you plan to do, as well as your feared outcomes, on the worksheet from exercise 4.2. Having a precise schedule for your experiment and writing down your initial expectations will increase the likelihood that you'll follow through on actually trying out your first experiments.

Some people report that they have difficulty starting behavioral experiments because they don't feel motivated to follow through. This reflects a common misconception about motivation. Contrary to popular opinion, action does not follow motivation, but rather precedes it. That is, you'll find that your motivation to complete behavioral experiments will increase *after* you've already started them, not before. This is similar to waiting for the motivation to exercise: it's better to push yourself to exercise at first, as once you've followed through, you'll be more motivated to keep exercising.

A final reason why some people have difficulty getting started on behavioral experiments has to do with the safety behavior of *partial commitment.* When we partially commit to people, situations, or tasks, we avoid the uncertainty of potentially failing, since, in general, we can't really make a mistake so long as we're not fully following through on something. However, partial commitment exacts a high cost, since we never get to fully own any successes either.

If you're someone who engages in partial commitment, you might find that this extends to your follow-through with this workbook. But if you got as far as deciding that worry was problematic enough in your life to warrant working through this book, then it's important to maximize your chances of success by giving it your best effort. Making the decision to fully invest in your own mental health and well-being is a behavioral experiment in itself, and one well worth trying!

## Experiments Don't Cause Anxiety

Whenever you choose a behavioral experiment to conduct, you do so based on the expectation that it will cause mild to moderate anxiety. However, it can sometimes be difficult to predict whether an uncertain situation will be as anxiety-provoking as you expect. If a behavioral experiment is not leading to any anxiety for you, it may be due to one of two reasons.

First, it might be because you picked something that is not challenging for you. Specifically, you're probably not anxious about the thought of your feared outcome actually occurring. For example, if your experiment was to go to the grocery store without a list, your feared outcome was likely that you would forget to buy something. If that outcome strikes you as a minor inconvenience but not something that would be upsetting or anxiety-provoking, then this isn't a good experiment for you. As such, when constructing your experiment, take a moment to look at your feared outcome and determine whether it leads to feelings of anxiety.

A second reason that a behavioral experiment is not causing anxiety has to do with the use of safety behaviors. As noted earlier, it's not uncommon for people to inadvertently replace one safety behavior with another. For example, if your experiment was to delegate a task to your spouse, you might have "undone" the experiment by watching over your spouse while the task was completed or having given precise instructions on how to complete the task beforehand. Both of these safety behaviors would have negated the experiment by reducing the uncertainty of the situation. To address this, take a moment to review your actions after completing a behavioral experiment to identify whether you engaged in an alternative safety behavior. Remember that behavioral experiments entail deliberately entering into an uncertain situation to observe the outcome, so attempts to reduce uncertainty interfere with this goal.

## Experiments Cause Too Much Anxiety

Just like you can overestimate how anxiety-provoking a particular behavioral experiment will be, you can also underestimate the resulting anxiety. Some experiments might not initially seem challenging but end up being far more difficult than you expect. If this is the case, you can either try another experiment (and save the more challenging ones for later) or make the current behavioral experiment more manageable. For example, if your experiment was to leave your phone in another room for two hours, you may have found that this was too difficult at first. In this case, you can lessen the time span of the experiment to whatever feels more manageable—an hour or half an hour.

Remember that the most important part of behavioral experiments is actually conducting them. So if you need to make an experiment easier in order to follow through with it, then that is the best course of action. You might find that you're able to increase the challenge of the experiment as time passes.

# In a Nutshell

In this chapter, we covered one of the most important strategies in this workbook for managing problematic worry. Behavioral experiments are designed to give you the tools to challenge your beliefs about the threat of uncertainty and reduce worry as a consequence. Here are some key points:

- A primary goal in managing worry is to reevaluate one's negative beliefs about uncertainty and develop more balanced beliefs. In order to change one's mind about the threat of uncertain situations, there needs to be compelling evidence against the accuracy of negative beliefs and in favor of more balanced beliefs.

- Safety behaviors are used to reduce anxiety and prevent feared outcomes. However, they also prevent the acquisition of evidence that might disprove negative beliefs about uncertainty, since they prevent us from finding out whether an uncertain situation would actually have had a negative outcome.

- By conducting behavioral experiments, you can directly test the accuracy of your beliefs about the threat of uncertain situations. When you complete a behavioral experiment, you are making a prediction about the outcome of an uncertain situation and then deliberately entering into that situation without using a safety behavior. This allows you to observe the actual outcome, as well as your ability to cope with negative outcomes should they occur.

- When conducting behavioral experiments, it's important to start small in order to not be overwhelmed by anxiety, to keep the stakes of the experiment low, and to expect to feel some anxiety when completing them. For your experiments to be maximally effective, you should record the results and conduct approximately three a week.

Behavioral experiments are one of the most powerful tools at your disposal to challenge your beliefs about the threat of uncertainty and, ultimately, to worry less. Be patient with yourself, as it can take time to gather evidence. With this in mind, the next chapter will help you further build upon the case against the threat of uncertainty as you continue to learn to develop a more balanced perspective on both the outcome of uncertain situations and your ability to handle any difficulties that might arise.

# CHAPTER 5

# Strengthening Your Tolerance for Uncertainty

In the previous chapter, we discussed the importance of engaging in behavioral experiments to test out your beliefs about the threat of uncertainty. At this point, you've had some time to gather new information about what actually happens in uncertain situations, and perhaps you're beginning to reconsider some of your negative beliefs about uncertainty. However, it can take time to gather compelling evidence necessary to change beliefs. As such, this chapter will focus on helping you conduct additional experiments to further test your beliefs. We'll also focus on strategies for building your overall tolerance for uncertainty by making facing uncertainty a part of your daily life. Developing more balanced beliefs and becoming more tolerant of uncertainty are key steps to reducing your worry and anxiety.

## Uncertainty Experiments

If you've been regularly conducting behavioral experiments, you've likely gathered some preliminary evidence about what actually happens when you face uncertainty: do uncertain situations lead to negative outcomes? What happens when you don't use your safety behaviors to make things more certain? Are you able to cope? By carrying out experiments, you get to truly test out whether your feared predictions come true and potentially gather some new information. Perhaps you're just starting to reevaluate your negative beliefs about uncertainty, or maybe you have already adopted more balanced beliefs about uncertainty. Regardless of where you are on that continuum, it generally takes a great deal of evidence to truly change beliefs.

That said, it's important to continue to engage in behavioral experiments to properly test out your beliefs about uncertainty. Because of this, the goal now becomes making sure you're facing uncertainty in a variety of contexts related to various worry themes, as well as facing more challenging situations.

## *Widen the Scope*

In chapter 4, you constructed behavioral experiments to target the worry themes most relevant to you. At this point, it's helpful to take a step back and notice if there are some areas that you haven't yet targeted. Perhaps you focused your behavioral experiments on uncertainty involving your health, but you haven't yet focused on uncertainty in work situations. You may also want to consider doing similar experiments, but in different contexts. For example, if you experimented with delegating household tasks to family members, you can now experiment with delegating work tasks to colleagues. The next exercise will help you widen the scope of your experiments by identifying areas you still need to target, as these are areas or contexts in which you have not yet had the chance to test out your beliefs about uncertainty.

# EXERCISE 5.1:
# Widening the Scope of Behavioral Experiments

The goal of this exercise is to help you develop new behavioral experiments by identifying uncertain situations you've not faced yet. Flip back to exercise 4.1 to identify the experiments that you rated as being anxiety-provoking: do they all fall into the same worry theme or multiple themes? If they fall under multiple worry themes, have you had the chance to conduct behavioral experiments related to all those themes yet? If not, now is the time.

Listed below are various worry themes. Place a check next to the themes that you worry about but that you have not yet targeted with any behavioral experiments or have targeted with only a limited number.

\_\_\_\_\_  Health/Physical Symptoms

\_\_\_\_\_  Danger/Safety

\_\_\_\_\_  Social Situations

\_\_\_\_\_  Work/School

\_\_\_\_\_  Interpersonal Relationships

\_\_\_\_\_  Daily Life Activities and Responsibilities

\_\_\_\_\_  Other: _____

After identifying relevant worry themes, use the list of potential behavioral experiments in exercise 4.1 to identify experiments in those areas you indicated would cause you anxiety. Given that you're just starting to test out your fears related to uncertainty in a new worry theme, it's better to start small with experiments that you rated as causing mild to moderate anxiety (scores of 3 or 4 out of 10) rather than trying something too difficult and getting overwhelmed.

If you're having trouble identifying new experiments, flip back to exercise 3.2 to identify some common safety behaviors you engage in and see if there are situations you're currently facing where you're using those safety behaviors. Try turning those situations into behavioral experiments. Remember, the goal is to pick situations in which you can refrain from engaging in a safety behavior, thereby deliberately experiencing some uncertainty.

List some new behavioral experiments in areas or contexts that you have not yet targeted or only tested out to a limited degree:

1. _____

_____

2. _____

_____

3. _____

_____

4. _____

_____

5. _____

_____

6. _____

_____

_____

We'll come back to this list shortly, so you don't actually need to complete any experiments just yet.

## Increase the Challenge

When we hold negative beliefs about uncertainty, facing uncertain situations through behavioral experiments feels threatening. But by starting with things that feel less scary, we can gradually build up to doing experiments that are more anxiety-provoking. At this point, you've probably been engaging in many behavioral experiments, and hopefully your confidence is growing. As such, you may be ready to try something more challenging or to conduct experiments with higher stakes. For example, if you experimented with having a brief unrehearsed conversation with a friend, you can make this experiment more challenging now by trying to have a brief unrehearsed conversation with your boss.

Some behavioral experiments are considered more challenging because the feared outcome is more severe, thus raising the stakes of the experiment. In having an unrehearsed conversation with a friend, a feared outcome might be that the conversation will be awkward. However, if you increase the stakes of this experiment by having an unrehearsed conversation with your boss, your feared outcome might be that you'll say the wrong thing, leading your boss to think you're incompetent and pass you over for a promotion. In this latter scenario, the stakes are obviously higher, making this new experiment more challenging.

## EXERCISE 5.2:
## Increasing the Challenge of Behavioral Experiments

The goal of this exercise is to develop more challenging behavioral experiments. To do this, flip back to exercise 4.1 to identify experiments that you indicated would likely cause you moderate to high levels of anxiety (scores of 5 or above). If you've been regularly conducting behavioral experiments, those you previously rated as highly anxiety-provoking might not seem so difficult now. But if you gave a potential experiment a high anxiety rating when you initially completed exercise 4.1 and have not actually conducted that experiment yet, consider adding it to your list below.

Another way to identify more challenging experiments is to review some that you've already completed, thinking about ways to change the parameters or raise the stakes. For example, if you initially went for a walk by yourself in a residential area during the day, a more challenging experiment would be walking in the same neighborhood in the evening.

Try to come up with a list of more challenging behavioral experiments:

1. _____

_____

2. _____

_____

3. _____

_____

4. _____

_____

5. _____

_____

6. _____

_____

We will come back to this list, so you don't need to complete any of these experiments just yet.

You should now have several ideas for your next round of behavioral experiments. The next exercise will help you turn those ideas into actual experiments. A few things about conducting behavioral experiments are worth repeating: First, a true experiment involves being clear about what you're doing and identifying your prediction about what you think will happen *before* you actually do it. Second, behavioral experiments should have outcomes that can be *observed* and *recorded*, thereby allowing you to determine whether the actual outcome differed from your feared outcome.

## EXERCISE 5.3:
# Constructing New Behavioral Experiments

With the ideas you came up with in exercises 5.1 and 5.2, you're now ready to construct new behavioral experiments. Looking at the potential experiments in both lists, consider which are the easiest to start with and pick three of them to try this week:

1. _____

_____

2. _____

_____

3. _____

_____

Record each experiment on the blank worksheet below (which is the same worksheet from exercise 4.2, available as a PDF at http://www.newharbinger.com/40064). Remember to complete the first two columns *before* you conduct your experiment and to fill in the last two columns *after* you've completed it.

| Experiment (what you will be doing) | Feared Outcome (what you are worried will happen) | Actual Outcome (what actually happened) | Coping (if the outcome was negative, how you handled it) |
|---|---|---|---|
| | | | |
| | | | |
| | | | |
| | | | |
| | | | |
| | | | |

## *Behavioral Experiments over Time*

Reevaluating your beliefs about the threat of uncertainty is such an important part of managing your worries that you'll want to make behavioral experiments a weekly habit—conducting two to three experiments per week for several weeks. Moreover, to ensure that you gather as much evidence as possible about the accuracy of your beliefs about uncertainty, widening the scope of your experiments by targeting different worry themes in different contexts and increasing the challenge and the stakes of your experiments will help you to get a richer and more complete picture of the actual threat of uncertainty.

Because the primary goal of behavioral experiments is to help you reevaluate the threat of uncertainty, it's important at the end of each week that you take stock of the information you gathered from your experiments and draw some conclusions. This next exercise will help you do that.

# EXERCISE 5.4:
# Summarizing Your Findings

As mentioned in chapter 4, it's a good idea to reflect on behavioral experiments and evaluate what the findings tell you about the outcomes of uncertain situations and your ability to handle negative outcomes should they arise. Accordingly, as you did in exercise 4.3, answer the following questions at the end of each week about the experiments you undertook that week (a copy of this questionnaire, first used in exercise 4.3, is available at http://www.newharbinger.com/40064). When you answer the fifth and final question, do so with *all* of the behavioral experiments you have completed since you started in mind.

1.  How often was the actual outcome positive or neutral? _____

_____

_____

2.  How often was the actual outcome negative? _____

_____

_____

3. When (and if) the outcomes were negative, were they as bad as expected? _____

_____

_____

4. When (and if) the outcomes were negative, how do you think you handled the situation?

_____

_____

5. So far, what are the results of the behavioral experiments telling you about the outcomes of uncertain situations and your ability to handle them?

_____

_____

_____

Remember that real change takes time and you're likely to think differently about uncertainty only once there is sufficient evidence against your negative beliefs. Holding balanced beliefs about uncertainty doesn't mean you view uncertain situations as positive. Rather, balanced beliefs involve the expectation that most uncertain situations will probably turn out fine and that when negative outcomes do occur, they're typically more of a hassle than a horror and we're generally able to cope with them.

# Tolerating Uncertainty Workouts

Until now, the focus has been on testing out the accuracy of your negative beliefs about the threat of uncertainty. At this point, you've hopefully accumulated some evidence suggesting that uncertain situations aren't as dangerous as you thought and that you're able to handle negative outcomes when they occur better than you expected. If we're less fearful of uncertainty, we can become more tolerant of it and, subsequently, less worried and anxious when faced with it. However, learning to tolerate uncertainty takes time. The goal now becomes less about testing out your fears and more about building your overall tolerance and acceptance of uncertainty.

## Building the Muscle of Uncertainty Tolerance

Learning to tolerate something is similar to the process of building a muscle. The more we work out a muscle, the stronger that muscle becomes. The same can be said for building our tolerance for something: the more we face it, the more tolerant of it we become. And just like a muscle we've built up, we have to continuously work it out in order to keep it strong. To maintain our tolerance for uncertainty, we need to make facing uncertainty a part of our daily life. With this in mind, we want to start thinking about tolerating uncertainty "exercises" or "workouts" you can consistently do to build and maintain your tolerance, just like a muscle.

When it comes to workouts for tolerating uncertainty, the focus shifts away from outcome (in this case, whether uncertain situations are dangerous and unmanageable) and more toward a willingness to face something that is uncertain regardless of the outcome. It's about going into an uncertain situation without knowing what's going to happen and being willing to sit with that uncertainty—even if sitting with it is uncomfortable or if the outcome ends up being negative. In addition, if we understand that uncertainty is an inevitable part of life and that being more tolerant of uncertainty will result in less anxiety and worry, then our goal becomes to accept and ultimately embrace uncertainty. In terms of completing tolerating uncertainty workouts, the goal is to face uncertain situations that pop up on a daily or weekly basis, identifying what you would normally do in those situations to make them more certain (safety behaviors), and then doing the opposite in order to sit with the uncertainty.

One thing that can be helpful in determining what to do in an uncertain situation is to act "as if" you are tolerant of uncertainty. That is, if you were someone who was tolerant of uncertainty, what would you do? For example, when faced with making a decision about a hotel for an upcoming trip, if you're acting "as if" you are tolerant of uncertainty, you may spend only thirty minutes researching hotels before making a decision rather than spending hours trying to be certain you got the "best" hotel. Similarly, when faced with some unexplained minor physical symptom (such as muscle pain), if you're acting "as if" you are tolerant of uncertainty, then you would not look up symptoms on the Internet. Instead, you would sit with the uncertainty of not knowing exactly what that symptom means.

# EXERCISE 5.5:
## Conducting Your Tolerating Uncertainty Workouts

This exercise helps you build your tolerance for uncertainty. On a daily or weekly basis, identify situations that pop up that allow you to sit with uncertainty by not engaging in safety behaviors. After you've completed a workout, use the worksheet provided to identify the situation you faced (uncertain situation), what you would typically do in that situation to make it more certain (typical safety behavior), what you did instead (tolerating uncertainty workout), and what happened (outcome). It can also be helpful to take note of how you felt during or after the workout. An example of a completed tolerating uncertainty workout worksheet is provided, as well as a blank worksheet (available as a PDF at http://www.newharbinger.com/40064) for your own use.

| Uncertain Situation | Typical Safety Behavior | Tolerating Uncertainty Workout (do the opposite—sit with the uncertainty) | Outcome (what happened and how you felt) |
|---|---|---|---|
| Bank left a message—not sure what they want | Not return the call | Phoned the bank back | Was anxious calling. Bank just wanted to let me know I was eligible for an increase on my credit card. Felt good that I called back. |
| Handing in a report for work—not sure if there are any mistakes | Check over report multiple times | Only checked over report once before handing it in | Felt anxious. Colleague pointed out a typo. Corrected it. Little embarrassed, but corrected the typo and resubmitted. |

| Uncertain Situation | Typical Safety Behavior | Tolerating Uncertainty Workout (do the opposite—sit with the uncertainty) | Outcome (what happened and how you felt) |
|---|---|---|---|
| | | | |
| | | | |
| | | | |
| | | | |
| | | | |
| | | | |

Keep in mind, the more tolerating uncertainty workouts you do, the more tolerant you'll become.

## *Taking Stock of Your Findings*

By now you've hopefully had significant opportunities to test out your beliefs about the threat of uncertainty, as well as the chance to build up your tolerance for uncertainty. Looking back across all of the behavioral experiments and tolerating uncertainty workouts you've completed, what have you learned? Is uncertainty as threatening as you thought? When uncertain situations had negative outcomes, were you able to cope? Do you look at uncertainty differently now? Do you find you're less worried or anxious? It's important to consolidate all of the evidence you've collected so far and use that information to draw some conclusions.

Without properly evaluating the evidence, we can fall into a type of selective thinking called *confirmation bias,* which is the tendency to interpret or recall information in a way that confirms our current belief system. This means that if you don't write down the outcomes of each experiment and workout and then give yourself the opportunity to summarize your findings, you're likely to interpret or recall outcomes that confirm your negative beliefs about uncertainty. For this reason, the next exercise is designed to help you take stock of your findings to date.

## EXERCISE 5.6:
# Taking Stock and Reviewing the Evidence

Armed with the information you obtained from all of the experiments and exercises you have completed to date, answer the following questions (available as a PDF questionnaire at http://www.newhar binger.com/40064):

1. How many behavioral experiments and tolerating uncertainty workouts have you completed so far?  _____

2. How many outcomes were positive or neutral?  _____

3. How many outcomes were negative?  _____

4. Of the negative outcomes, how many were as bad or worse than you expected?  _____

5. How many times did you cope with a negative outcome?  _____

6. Of those times you had to cope with a negative outcome, how many times did you feel you coped well with the situation?  _____

Take some time now to consider the ways in which the work you have done so far has impacted you. You may have noticed that your perspective on things has shifted. You may be less fearful of uncertain situations and have actually noticed a reduction in your worry. Use the following questions to help you take stock of any changes you have undergone.

Do you find uncertainty as threatening as you did before? _____

_____

Are you more willing to face uncertain situations? _____

_____

_____

Have you been engaging in fewer safety behaviors? _____

_____

_____

Do you have more confidence in your ability to cope with or handle negative outcomes?

_____

_____

Are you worrying less or feeling less anxious? _____

_____

_____

Have other people commented on changes they are seeing in you? _____

_____

_____

Many people discover that their long-held beliefs about the threat of uncertainty are inaccurate. You may have realized this too. Although negative outcomes do occur, they often don't occur as frequently as we expect, they're typically more of a hassle than a horror, and we're generally able to cope.

You may have also discovered that facing uncertainty can be quite rewarding. You may have felt proud of yourself for facing something challenging or coping well with a difficult situation. Unfortunately, we rob ourselves of the opportunity to learn what we're actually capable of when we constantly avoid uncertainty.

In addition, you may have experienced a number of very positive outcomes that you wouldn't have discovered had you not faced an uncertain situation. For instance, if you had not accepted an invitation to a friend's party, you may have missed a really fun time or the opportunity to meet someone new.

Noticing changes can be a big motivator for continuing to face uncertainty. If you haven't yet noticed any changes, give it more time. You may also benefit from some of the next chapters that target specific problem areas.

# In a Nutshell

In this chapter, you had the opportunity to conduct additional behavioral experiments to further test your beliefs about the threat of uncertainty and build your tolerance for uncertainty by engaging in tolerating uncertainty workouts. Here are some key points:

- To increase the depth of evidence against negative beliefs about uncertainty, it's important to widen the scope of your experiments, increase the challenge, and raise the stakes.

- To widen the scope of your behavioral experiments, target all of the worry themes relevant to you, particularly those that haven't been incorporated into your experiments so far.

- It's important to start conducting behavioral experiments that are more challenging. This includes experiments you initially identified as more anxiety-provoking, as well as experiments that have the potential for more significant negative outcomes (higher stakes).

- Whereas behavioral experiments involve testing out your beliefs about the threat of uncertain situations, "uncertainty workouts" involve building your tolerance to uncertainty in daily life. This means consistently facing uncertain situations and sitting with the uncertainty in order to build tolerance for those situations.

- It's important to take stock of the findings from behavioral experiments and tolerating uncertainty workouts. Many people discover that their beliefs about uncertainty are inaccurate. More often than not, uncertain situations turn out fine. Even when a negative outcome occurs, it's more of a hassle than a horror, and we can cope.

At this point, you've hopefully started to develop more balanced beliefs about uncertainty and have been working on building your tolerance for uncertainty. In the upcoming chapters, you'll have the opportunity to further build upon and consolidate your gains.

# CHAPTER 6

# Facing the Uncertainty in Perfectionism

Throughout our lives, we are encouraged to challenge ourselves and excel. As young children, we're monitored and corrected as we develop our language and interpersonal skills. Once we start school, we're regularly graded and critiqued. Evaluations and comparisons continue as we pursue higher education and career advancement. We're continuously setting expectations and assessing our ability to meet them.

In a society that values excellence, we're often driven to set higher and higher standards as a way to achieve "success," and pursuing excellence has many payoffs: we can achieve great things and be rewarded for our accomplishments. However, there is a point at which our standards may become impossible to meet, and our attempts to achieve them come at too great a cost.

In this chapter, we'll explore a common theme related to problematic worry: perfectionism. Although you might worry about different things, your worries may in fact revolve around the larger theme of perfectionism. For this reason, this chapter will focus on targeting worries related to perfectionism. You'll learn the difference between healthy high standards and problematic perfectionistic expectations, how perfectionism is connected to intolerance of uncertainty, and specific strategies for targeting worries related to perfectionism.

## What Is Perfectionism?

Most people want to excel in their lives. By setting high standards, we may be more motivated to push ourselves to perform at peak levels to accomplish goals. For example, by pushing ourselves to attain straight A's in school, we might win a scholarship. Or by setting high expectations at work, we might get promoted. Setting high standards and attempting to improve our performance is not the same as being perfectionistic.

Perfectionism has been defined in many ways, but it typically involves setting excessively high standards, believing that doing something perfectly is not only possible but necessary, being overly self-critical of mistakes, and regarding anything short of perfection as unacceptable (Frost et al. 1990; Obsessive Compulsive Cognitions Working Group 1997). Unfortunately, being perfectionistic means setting such high standards that either we're unlikely to attain them or they can be met only with great difficulty or at a great cost.

## Healthy High Standards vs. Perfectionism

Whether a personal standard is healthy or perfectionistic depends on a number of factors (see Antony and Swinson 2009; Burns 1980; Shafran, Egan, and Wade 2010; Hamacheck 1978).

First, is the standard *realistic and attainable*? Appropriate high standards are typically achievable, whereas perfectionistic expectations are extremely unlikely to be met.

Second, what are the *consequences* of holding such a standard? Healthy high standards have benefits, such as improved performance, with acceptable costs. It may take time and effort to achieve them, but not an excessive amount and not at the expense of other things in your life, such as relationships or your mental health. On the other hand, perfectionistic expectations may have benefits, such as enhanced performance, but have adverse consequences. For example, trying to achieve extreme expectations is exhausting and time-consuming and can actually impede performance.

Third, is the standard or expectation *rigid* or *flexible*? With perfectionistic expectations, there are no exceptions and anything less than perfect is unacceptable. In contrast, healthy high standards are flexible and can include exceptions, such that standards can be modified when appropriate or necessary.

Finally, what is the *basis of one's self-worth*? In terms of healthy high standards, self-worth is based on more than one's achievements or ability to meet expectations. Alternatively, perfectionism involves basing self-worth almost exclusively on one's achievements and ability to meet excessively high standards.

An example can highlight these differences. Jada believes it's important to avoid mistakes at work because that could be perceived as a sign of incompetence, and she could be passed over for promotions. As a result, Jada spends a great deal of time and effort trying to ensure that her work is flawless. When she has a meeting or presentation, she spends hours preparing and excessively rehearses what she's going to say. She tries to anticipate every question she could be asked in order to formulate the "correct" response. She seeks excessive reassurance from colleagues that her answers are accurate. In addition, she spends a significant amount of time drafting and reviewing e-mails to avoid mistakes.

Despite her efforts, Jada is unable to anticipate every question, and at times she struggles to answer them. Although she rechecks her e-mails, she periodically uses incorrect grammar or misspells a word. The additional work she puts into preparing for meetings is taking a significant toll on her, as she is exhausted and rarely has time to spend with her husband. Recently, her mother became ill, and she was unable to put as much time as usual into a presentation. As a consequence, she felt "off her game." She spent hours ruminating about how the presentation went and chastised herself for her less-than-perfect performance.

Moreover, Jada applies the same standards to all situations. For example, she spends the same amount of time checking for mistakes in an e-mail arranging a meeting with a colleague as she does preparing an important proposal for a client. At the end of the day, Jada considers herself a "failure" for her inability to meet her expectations.

In Jada's situation, her expectations aren't realistic and attainable. No matter how much time and energy she puts into avoiding mistakes, her performance is not perfect. In terms of consequences, although Jada gets praised for the high quality of her work, trying to meet her own expectations comes at a high cost. Her efforts to avoid mistakes are time-consuming, result in heightened stress, and negatively affect her relationships. Jada's expectations are also rigid and inflexible. She was unable to modify her expectations when her mother got sick, which left her feeling overwhelmed and upset. Additionally, she seems unable to recognize that applying the same excessive standards to all situations is not very efficient. Finally, Jada bases her self-worth almost exclusively on her achievements and ability (or inability) to meet her expectations. Because her expectations are so excessive and rigid, she often fails to meet them and, as a result, sees herself as a failure. Jada's expectations are more perfectionistic than healthy and more costly than beneficial.

# The Problem with Perfectionism

Perfectionism takes a large toll—it is stressful and exhausting, requiring a great deal of time and energy. Not only that, but when we're consumed with trying to meet perfectionistic expectations, we use up a great deal of our resources, leaving us with little patience and heightened irritability, so other areas of our life suffer. We may have little time and energy left over to invest in relationships or recreational activities, and we may struggle to give ourselves permission to relax. Perfectionism can also impact our mood. With standards so difficult to meet, we're constantly falling short, which becomes demoralizing and depressing. Finally, perfectionism is likely to result in heightened worry and anxiety; with so many things to make perfect, there's lots to worry about. And the more worried and anxious we become, the more difficult it becomes to focus and the more our ability to meet our goals and expectations may be impaired.

## Perfectionism and Worry

The relationship between perfectionism and worry has been well established. Research has shown that perfectionism is linked to anxiety (Egan, Wade, and Shafron 2011; Kawamura et al. 2001), various anxiety disorders (Antony et al. 1998), and excessive worry (Handley et al. 2014; Santanello and Gardner 2007; Stöber and Joormann 2001). Since perfectionists consider anything less than perfect unacceptable, it's not surprising that these individuals worry about the tasks they need to accomplish and their ability to meet their expectations.

Given the link between perfectionism and worry, combined with the cost of being perfectionistic, it's important to figure out the degree to which you hold perfectionistic expectations. This next exercise will help you identify whether you're a perfectionist.

---

# EXERCISE 6.1:
# Are You a Perfectionist?

Read over the following statements and provide a number between 1 and 3 indicating how typical the statement is of you.

**Scoring:**

1 = Not typical of me

2 = Somewhat typical of me

3 = Very typical of me

1. _____ I set high standards for myself that are often hard to meet.

2. _____ Others tell me that my standards are too high.

3. _____ I worry about making mistakes or not doing well.

4. _____ I'm very hard on myself when I don't meet my expectations.

5. _____ I often feel anxious, worried, and frustrated when trying to reach my goals.

6. _____ I tend to compare myself to others.

7. _____ I'm extremely critical of myself when I make a mistake.

8. _____ I tend to redo things or spend too much time on tasks.

9. _____ My standards are so high that I often procrastinate completing tasks because of the amount of time it would take to complete them.

10. _____ I typically feel like I should have done more to meet my goals.

11. _____ I tend to seek reassurance that I've done things correctly.

12. _____ I don't give myself credit for my accomplishments.

13. _____ I avoid trying new things because I'm not sure I'll be good at them.

14. _____ I'm uncomfortable when things aren't "just right."

15. _____ I recheck things to make sure I've done them correctly.

16. _____ I believe that anything less than perfect is a failure.

17. _____ I'm afraid to appear incompetent.

18. _____ I tend to prefer to do things my way and don't trust others to do them correctly.

If you scored a 2 or 3 on at least 9 of the above statements, you likely struggle with perfectionism. In general, the more items that you scored as either "somewhat" or "very typical" of you, the more perfectionistic you may be and the more likely you are to have worries under the theme of perfectionism.

---

## Life Areas Impacted by Perfectionism

Perfectionistic standards and expectations can be applied to numerous life areas. Some people hold excessively high standards in just one or two areas of their life (such as work or school), while other people find that perfectionism is an issue in most areas of their life (Shafran, Egan, and Wade 2010). Common areas in which perfectionism can lead to problems include:

*Work/school:* Although most people want to do well at their jobs or in their studies, some people set excessively high standards. You may believe your work must be completed correctly and flawlessly. You may take an excessive amount of time properly filling out forms or perfectly wording an e-mail. Receiving feedback that's not completely positive is deemed a "failure," and anything less than a perfect grade or performance review is considered unacceptable.

*Social situations:* Some people have extremely high expectations of themselves in social situations. You might believe that you should always be articulate and well spoken, never making mistakes when speaking with others. You may be concerned about expressing yourself perfectly in e-mails or texts. Some people worry about making social events perfect, like excessively preparing for a casual get-together to ensure that the food and entertainment are perfect.

*Physical appearance:* For some people, perfectionistic standards are applied to their physical appearance. In this case, you may be overly concerned about aspects of your body, such as your weight. Some people put a great deal of effort into their appearance and spend excessive amounts of time trying to get their hair, makeup, or outfit "just right."

*Neatness, cleanliness, and organization:* Some individuals spend hours cleaning and tidying, insist on doing or organizing things a certain way, avoid delegating tasks to others, and feel uncomfortable when things don't look perfect. They may make excessive to-do lists and spend a great deal of time trying to complete those lists.

Having perfectionist expectations in various life areas is likely to lead to worries about meeting those expectations. The next exercise is designed to help you figure out where perfectionistic worries pop up in your life.

# EXERCISE 6.2:
# Identifying Your Perfectionism Worries

Take some time to think about whether perfectionism is a problem for you in the life areas listed below. Read over the examples and check off every category that reflects your worries. You can also refer to your responses on the worry tracking sheets from chapters 1 and 3 to help you complete this.

_____ **Work or School**

Do you constantly worry about your grades or performance at work? Do you become extremely disappointed when you don't perform at the level you think you should? Do even simple tasks or assignments take a long time to complete? Are you excessively concerned about making mistakes? Do you tend to recheck or redo things to make sure you've done them perfectly?

_____ **Social Situations**

Are you overly concerned about making mistakes when interacting with others? Are you concerned about mispronouncing words or saying the wrong thing? Are you worried about perfectly expressing yourself in e-mails or texts? Do you spend excessive amounts of time planning and preparing for social events in order to make things perfect?

_____ **Physical Appearance**

Do you worry excessively about your appearance? Do you always feel like you could look better? Do you spend a lot of time trying to get your hair, makeup, and clothes "just right"?

_____ **Neatness, Cleanliness, and Organization**

Do you spend a great deal of time cleaning and tidying? Do you have very set ways for ordering and arranging things? Do you feel uncomfortable when things don't look perfect or aren't "just right"? Do you prefer to do things yourself so they can be done correctly? Do you make excessive to-do lists?

_____ **Other Perfectionism Worries**

_____

_____

Knowing what perfectionism worries are problematic for you will help you design exercises to address these worries in the latter part of this chapter.

## Uncertainty and Perfectionism

Both intolerance of uncertainty and perfectionism are linked to problematic worry and anxiety. This isn't surprising given that perfectionism is about trying to make things perfect, and when things are perfect, they're certain. Because of this, perfectionism can be viewed as a way of trying to avoid uncertainty. By setting excessively high standards and attempting to avoid mistakes, we're potentially trying to make outcomes less uncertain. If we're intolerant of uncertainty, then we're more likely to adopt perfectionistic standards as a way to minimize or avoid the uncertainties in life. Alternatively, if we're perfectionists who view anything less than perfect as unacceptable, we would expect to be intolerant of the uncertainty around our ability to meet our standards.

In chapter 2, we introduced the idea that people who are intolerant of uncertainty hold negative beliefs about uncertainty. Perfectionism worries are related to fears about making mistakes and falling short of expectations (Conroy, Kaye, and Fifer 2007; Frost et al. 1990). If you believe that anything less than perfect is unacceptable, then you probably hold negative beliefs about the consequences of making mistakes or being imperfect. For example, let's say that Caleb decides to host a friend's birthday party. He holds perfectionistic expectations and worries about getting all the details just right—such as invitations and decorations—and ensuring that his home is spotless and the food is delicious. He believes that if things aren't perfect, his friends will think less of him. As a result, he's quite anxious about the party.

How we react and deal with uncertain situations, like hosting a party, depends not only on our expectations, but also on our beliefs about what will happen if those expectations aren't met. Perfectionism worries are related to the following negative beliefs about the uncertainty around the consequences of making mistakes and falling short of expectations:

*Mistakes or imperfection will lead to negative outcomes.* When we hold perfectionistic expectations, we may believe that making mistakes or not doing things perfectly will result in negative outcomes. If you make a spelling mistake in an e-mail to your friend, for instance, you may assume she'll notice and think less of you. Or you may believe that if you don't put a lot of time and effort into a report, the quality of the work will be significantly reduced.

*Negative outcomes will be catastrophic.* Not only do people with perfectionism worries believe that situations in which they fail to meet their expectations will turn out negatively, they also tend to anticipate that the outcome will be horrible. For example, if you don't do an outstanding job on a project, you might assume you'll get fired. Or you may believe that if you aren't perfectly groomed at all times, people will think you're a slob and no one will ever be interested in dating you.

*We'll be unable to cope with negative outcomes.* Finally, we may believe that when an imperfect situation turns out negatively, we'll be unable to cope. For instance, you may believe that if you fail to clean your kitchen perfectly, not only would others notice, but you would be overwhelmed with shame and embarrassment and unable to deal with those feelings.

If we believe that making mistakes and being imperfect will lead to negative consequences, then it's not surprising that we might use specific safety behaviors to reduce the chances of making mistakes or being imperfect and to become more certain about the outcome.

## Safety Behaviors and Perfectionism

As previously described, safety behaviors are deliberate actions taken to reduce anxiety in feared situations and to prevent feared outcomes. When it comes to worries involving perfectionism, these behaviors are an attempt to make things perfect and achieve our own rigorous standards. Unfortunately, safety behaviors prevent us from learning what happens when we do make mistakes or fall short of expectations. We never get to learn that perhaps being imperfect isn't that problematic.

The next step is to figure out what safety behaviors you engage in so that you can conduct behavioral experiments designed to discover what actually happens when you deliberately let go of perfectionistic standards.

# EXERCISE 6.3:
# Identifying Your Perfectionism Safety Behaviors

In the following list of common safety behaviors related to perfectionism, place a check next to all the categories you engage in.

_____ **Excessive Checking**

Checking and rechecking things to ensure that you haven't made any mistakes and that things are "perfect" or have been done according to your rigorous standards.

_____ **Excessive Reassurance Seeking**

Asking others to ensure you have done things correctly or assure you that you've met a particular standard; for example, you might repeatedly ask others whether you handled a situation well or did a good job.

_____ **Excessive Preparation**

Spending an excessive amount of time and energy preparing for things or completing tasks; for example, preparing excessively for meetings, presentations, or social events, focusing on minor details, or taking a long time to complete simple tasks.

_____ **Excessive Slowness**

Completing tasks slowly and cautiously to ensure they've been done correctly and to your standards; for example, you might read very slowly or repeatedly reread the same paragraph to make sure you haven't missed anything.

_____ **Redoing Things**

Redoing or repeating tasks to make sure they're done correctly, such as recleaning the house when it doesn't precisely meet your standards.

_____ **Doing Everything Yourself**

Refusing to delegate tasks and doing everything yourself to be entirely sure they're done correctly and according to your standards.

**_____ Avoidance**

Avoiding situations or tasks where you're not certain you won't make a mistake or meet your precise expectations; for example, avoiding cleaning the house because you're worried you won't be able to clean it to your standards.

**_____ Procrastination**

Any attempts to delay doing things where you may make a mistake or be unable to reach your expectations; for example, you might procrastinate completing a report or assignment in order to feel less responsible for it and to have an excuse for not having completed it perfectly.

**_____ Other Safety Behaviors Related to Perfectionism**

Write down any other behaviors you use to avoid making mistakes or to attempt to make things perfect:

_____

_____

If you found it challenging to identify safety behaviors related to perfectionism, it can be helpful to review your responses to exercise 3.1 to get some ideas.

Now that you have a better sense of the types of perfectionism-related safety behaviors that you use, it's time to test out your fears related to perfectionism.

# Behavioral Experiments Targeting Perfectionism

Safety behaviors can prevent us from figuring out whether our feared beliefs about uncertainty are true. In the case of worries involving perfectionism, safety behaviors prevent us from discovering whether making mistakes leads to catastrophic outcomes, whether others will notice and subsequently view our imperfections (and us) in a negative way, or whether putting in less effort leads to reductions in overall performance. We also never get the opportunity to try new things where expertise isn't already present. This robs us of opportunities to discover new interests and do things simply for enjoyment, which can enrich our lives. Because of this, it's important to test out the accuracy of your beliefs about perfectionism through behavioral experiments.

# Constructing Perfectionism Behavioral Experiments

To plan behavioral experiments for perfectionism worries, you need to identify situations for which you have a specific prediction about what will happen if you don't engage in safety behaviors designed to prevent making mistakes or to meet perfectionistic expectations. The following questions can help you assess the accuracy of your beliefs after you complete a behavioral experiment:

1. Did the situation turn out negatively?

2. If the outcome was negative, how bad was it?

3. If it was negative, how did you handle it?

Let's use an example. Abigail believes that if she's not well spoken, her friends will think badly of her and be less likely to engage her in conversation in the future. As a result, she rehearses what she's going to say before she says it to avoid mistakes in her speech. A good behavioral experiment for Abigail would be to have a conversation with a friend and sit with uncertainty by not rehearsing what she's going to say. This allows her to test out what happens when she doesn't try to make the conversation perfect and whether that leads to a negative outcome, such as her friends being less likely to discuss things with her in the future.

Using the example of Abigail, she may report the following after meeting a friend:

1. Did the situation turn out negatively? *Yes, I stumbled over my words a couple times and at one point lost my train of thought. There were some awkward pauses, and my friend looked a little uncomfortable at one point.*

2. If the outcome was negative, how bad was it? *It wasn't that bad. We still had a good conversation, and my friend still seemed to enjoy herself.*

3. If it was negative, how did you handle it? *When I stumbled over my words and lost my train of thought, I tried to keep going and think of other things to talk about in the moment. I actually felt like I could follow the conversation a little better since I wasn't so focused on trying to think about what to say next. I think I handled things pretty well.*

By conducting this experiment, Abigail is able to evaluate some of her beliefs about the uncertainty of being imperfect. In this case, although the conversation wasn't perfect, she managed to get through it. However, it'll be important for Abigail to conduct multiple experiments to properly assess whether her beliefs are accurate or whether they need to be modified. Now it's time to start constructing your own behavioral experiments related to perfectionism.

# EXERCISE 6.4:
# Identifying Your Own Perfectionism Experiments

Read through the different types of experiments targeting perfectionism worries presented below. Next to each potential experiment, write down the level of anxiety (from 0 to 10, with 0 = no anxiety and 10 = severe anxiety) you would expect to feel faced with that situation. You can also come up with your own experiments (using exercise 6.3 for ideas if you wish).

### Experiments Targeting Work/School

_____ Show up 5–10 minutes late for work or class

_____ Start a task when you're not completely sure how to do it

_____ Answer a question in a meeting/class without being completely sure you have the correct answer

_____ Give an incorrect answer in a meeting/class

_____ Make a spelling mistake in an e-mail

_____ Don't recheck an e-mail before sending it

_____ Delegate a task to a coworker

_____ Complete a simple task/assignment quickly without reviewing it

_____ Purposely make a minor mistake or leave something incomplete on a small task/assignment

_____ Spend less time on a project/presentation than you usually would

_____ Don't seek reassurance about your work

What are other work/school-related experiments you can think of?

_____

_____

## Experiments Targeting Social Situations

_____ Lose your place when telling a story

_____ Mispronounce a word

_____ Show up 5–10 minutes late to meet a friend or for an appointment

_____ Don't review an e-mail/text before sending it

_____ Purposely allow pauses while having a conversation

_____ Share something that makes you feel weak or "imperfect" (that you're tired or stressed)

_____ Discuss a topic that you're not 100 percent knowledgeable about

_____ Have a conversation without rehearsing what you're going to say

_____ Don't excessively plan for a social event

What are other experiments related to social situations you can think of?

_____

_____

## Experiments Targeting Physical Appearance

_____ Skip a day or two of washing your hair

_____ Go out without styling your hair

_____ Go out without makeup

_____ Wear a mismatched outfit

_____ Go out in sweats or with something that has a stain on it

_____ Spend less time picking out an outfit (if you normally spend 30 minutes, try 15)

What are other experiments related to physical appearance you can think of?

_____

_____

## Experiments Targeting Neatness, Cleanliness, and Organization

_____ Leave part of your house slightly messy (like dishes in the sink)

_____ Skip a day of cleaning

_____ Only do a quick clean before having someone over

_____ Don't clean before having someone over

_____ Don't plan every detail of a dinner party/social event

_____ Delegate a task (such as folding laundry) to someone else

_____ Mix clothes around in your closet or leave your closet a little messy

What are other experiments related to neatness, cleanliness, and organization you can think of?

_____

_____

## Other Types of Perfectionism Experiments

_____ Try an activity you've never done before (yoga class, mountain climbing, painting)

_____ Engage in an activity you know you're not good at

Any other experiments you can think of?

_____

_____

In the next section, you'll use this information to help you design some initial experiments.

## Tips for Developing Useful Experiments

In chapter 4, we presented a detailed list of tips to develop good experiments. Here are a few of them for review:

- Be clear about what you're doing and identify your prediction about what you think will happen *before* actually doing it.

- Start small with experiments that are not too challenging or overwhelming to complete.

- Conduct multiple experiments. If you complete an experiment only once or twice, you're more likely to attribute your results to luck or chance.

---

## EXERCISE 6.5:
## Conducting Your Perfectionism Behavioral Experiments

Now that you have some ideas for behavioral experiments, it's time to start planning and conducting your own. Using the list of potential experiments from exercise 6.4, pick two or three that you expect to cause you mild or moderate anxiety (scores of 3 or 4) and commit to conducting them this week:

1. _____

2. _____

3. _____

For each experiment, use the worksheet that follows, for which both a completed sample and a blank version (also available as a PDF at http://www.newharbinger.com/40064) are provided. Remember to complete the first two columns *before* you conduct your experiment and to fill in the last two columns *after* you've completed it.

| Targeting Perfectionism Experiment (what you will be doing) | Feared Outcome (what you are worried will happen) | Actual Outcome (what actually happened) | Coping (if the outcome was negative, how you handled it) |
|---|---|---|---|
| *Leave house without doing hair or makeup* | *Will run into someone I know. They'll notice my appearance and think I'm a mess. It'll feel awkward.* | *Didn't run into anyone I knew. No one else seemed to really notice my appearance.* | *Not necessary* |
| *Show up 10 minutes late for lunch with my cousin* | *Cousin will be upset. Lunch will be strained. She'll continue to be upset with me.* | *Cousin seemed a little annoyed and wasn't talkative at first. I felt bad.* | *Gave a sincere apology. Rest of lunch was okay. Still had a nice time. Spoke later in the week and everything seemed fine.* |

| Targeting Perfectionism Experiment (what you will be doing) | Feared Outcome (what you are worried will happen) | Actual Outcome (what actually happened) | Coping (if the outcome was negative, how you handled it) |
|---|---|---|---|
| | | | |
| | | | |
| | | | |
| | | | |
| | | | |
| | | | |

We recommend completing two to three behavioral experiments a week for at least a month. You can come up with new experiments each week or complete the same experiment multiple times. Make sure to target all the areas of your life where you hold perfectionistic expectations. After each week of completing experiments, it's important to review the evidence to assess the accuracy of your beliefs about perfectionism, which the next exercise will help you do.

## EXERCISE 6.6:
## Summarizing the Findings of Your Perfectionism Experiments

It's important to reflect on your behavioral experiments and evaluate what the findings tell you about the outcomes of uncertainty around making mistakes and falling short of perfectionism. At the end of each week, fill out this questionnaire (also available at http://www.newharbinger.com/40064) about the perfectionism experiments you conducted that week. When you answer the final question, make sure to consider *all* of the perfectionism behavioral experiments you have completed thus far.

1.  How often was the actual outcome positive or neutral? _____

_____

_____

2.  How often was the actual outcome negative? _____

_____

_____

3.  When (and if) the outcomes were negative, were they as bad as expected? _____

_____

_____

4.  When (and if) the outcomes were negative, how do you think you handled the situation?

_____

_____


5.  So far, what are the results of your behavioral experiments telling you about your beliefs about making mistakes or falling short of perfection and your ability to handle those situations?

_____

_____

_____


## Taking Stock of Your Findings

By now you've hopefully had significant opportunities to test out your beliefs about uncertainty around imperfection. Looking back across all of the perfectionism-related behavioral experiments you've conducted, what have you learned? Do you always make mistakes when you don't engage in safety behaviors? Even when you do make mistakes or fall short of your expectations, do things turn out badly? Do people always notice when you make a mistake? If people do notice, has that resulted in negative consequences? If you revised your expectations, did that lead to a reduction in your overall performance? Did changing some of your expectations result in less time, energy, and stress?

With all the information you have so far, do you look at perfectionism differently now? And most importantly, do you find that you're less worried and anxious? It's important to draw some overall conclusions from all of the information you've gathered.

_____

_____

_____

# EXERCISE 6.7:
# Perfectionism: Reviewing the Evidence

Reflect on the information you've obtained from all of your perfectionism behavioral experiments and answer the following questions (a PDF of this questionnaire is available at http://www.newharbinger.com/40064):

1.  Do you find making mistakes or not meeting perfectionistic standards as threatening as you did before?

_____

_____

2.  Have you been engaging in fewer safety behaviors related to avoiding mistakes or trying to make things perfect?

_____

_____

3.  Are you more willing to make mistakes and allow things to be imperfect than you were before?

_____

_____

4.   Do you have more confidence in your ability to cope with or handle situations when you do make mistakes or are less than perfect?

_____

_____

_____

5.   Has reducing perfectionistic expectations resulted in a significant reduction in your overall performance or the quality of your work?

_____

_____

_____

6.   Are you worrying less or feeling less anxious? _____

_____

_____

7.   Have other people commented on changes they are seeing in you? _____

_____

_____

Noticing changes can be a big motivator for continuing to modify your behavior and test out your beliefs about perfectionism. If you haven't noticed changes yet, you probably just need more time and practice. If you've begun to develop new beliefs around perfectionism, the next section will help you develop healthier standards, which can result in less worry and anxiety.

# Developing Healthy High Standards

It can be challenging to give up long-held personal standards and expectations, even with new evidence that they may not be appropriate. Because of this, it's helpful to compare the various costs and benefits of continuing to maintain your perfectionistic standards versus adopting new alternative high standards.

---

## EXERCISE 6.8:
## Costs and Benefits of Perfectionistic
## vs. Healthy High Standards

Now that you've had a chance to test out some of your beliefs about perfectionism, an important next step involves contrasting the consequences of perfectionistic versus high standards. Take some time to list the costs and benefits of each in the table below. Consider the following:

- Ability to consistently meet expectations (do your standards help you or hinder you from actually meeting expectations?)

- Time, energy, and effort necessary to meet goals

- Reaction to meeting goals (how do you feel about yourself when you meet or don't meet your goals/expectations?)

- Ability to maintain high level of performance (are you able to get everything done?)

- Impact on other parts of life (relationships, downtime, recreational interests)

- Impact on mental and physical health (stress, exhaustion, anxiety, worry)

|  | Benefits (pros) | Costs (cons) |
|---|---|---|
| *Perfectionistic Standards* | | |
| *Healthy High Standards* | | |

Hopefully, you've begun to notice that healthy high standards can help you achieve your goals without the costs of perfectionistic expectations. Check out the next section for a review of some of the things that differentiate healthy high standards from perfectionistic expectations.

There are many benefits to adopting healthy high standards, as they can allow you to aim for excellence without the burden of trying to be perfect. Although we contrasted the difference between healthy high standards and perfectionistic expectations at the beginning of this chapter, review the table below, which revisits the comparison, especially since you may have some new evidence suggesting that it's not worth maintaining your perfectionistic expectations.

| Healthy High Standards/Expectations | Perfectionistic Standards/Expectations |
| --- | --- |
| High but realistic and achievable goals/standards/expectations, which can be consistently met | Extremely high goals/standards/expectations, which are often not met |
| Motivation: desire for improvement | Motivation: fear of failure |
| Requires hard work, but manageable | Requires a great deal of energy and extremely time-consuming |
| Get pleasure from meeting goals | Never feel satisfied |
| Bounce back easily from mistakes and "failures"; see mistakes as part of life and a learning opportunity | Struggle to bounce back from mistakes and "failures"; see mistakes as evidence of not being worthy or competent |
| React positively to constructive criticism | React negatively to any kind of criticism |
| Flexible—exceptions and quotas for mistakes Recognition that not all situations require the same high standards and acceptance of circumstances that may prevent standards from being met | Rigid—no exceptions and no quotas for mistakes Same standards applied to all situations regardless of importance or circumstances |
| Confident, encouraging, self-compassionate | Full of self-doubt, self-critical |
| Self-worth based on more than achievements | Self-worth based on achievements |
| Leads to greater emotional wellness | Negatively impacts mental health; results in stress, exhaustion, irritability, worry, anxiety, and depression |

(See Antony and Swinson 2009; Burns 1980; Shafran, Egan, and Wade 2010; Hamacheck 1978.)

With all the information you've discovered about perfectionism in this chapter, you're hopefully ready to start adopting healthier expectations and, by doing so, take another step toward reducing your worry and anxiety.

# Learning to Be "Good Enough"

One of the problems with perfectionistic standards is that they're applied to every situation. Given that not all situations are created equal, it's a good idea to learn to become more *selective* with your standards and to figure out when "good enough" standards are more appropriate. For example, does folding laundry really need the same level of precision as completing your tax forms, or does texting a close friend require the same attention to detail as writing a cover letter for your dream job?

You may want to apply high standards for things that are important to you (studying for a final exam, preparing for a very important presentation) or when a negative outcome could be costly (not using precise measurements when ordering new kitchen cabinetry, not reading the dosage instructions on medication for your child). But aiming for "good enough" when outcomes are less likely to be negative or to have a significant impact if things aren't completed at a high standard (texting a close friend, picking an outfit to run an errand) can save considerable time and energy and, ultimately, reduce anxiety.

## *Building the Muscle of "Good Enough"*

If you're used to applying perfectionistic expectations, embracing a "good enough" approach can be challenging. Learning to apply new standards is similar to the process of building a muscle. The more we work out a muscle, the stronger that muscle becomes. The same can be said for setting "good enough" standards: the more we do it, the easier it becomes. And just like a muscle that we've built up, we have to continuously exercise it to keep it strong.

Start thinking about workouts you can consistently do to build and maintain your tolerance of standards that are sufficient, not perfect. The goal is to identify situations that don't require high standards, either because the risk of a negative outcome is unlikely or the severity or cost of a negative outcome would be negligible.

The types of tasks that might qualify for "good enough" standards include:

- Texting/e-mailing a close friend or family member

- Phoning a close friend or family member

- E-mailing a colleague to set up a meeting

- Cleaning your kitchen before leaving for work

- Cleaning your house before having close family over

- Folding laundry

- Doing your hair or makeup to run a quick errand

- Getting dressed to run a quick errand

- Talking to baristas/cashiers

- Choosing a restaurant or movie

# EXERCISE 6.9:
## "Good Enough" Workouts

On a daily or weekly basis, identify situations where you can apply "good enough" standards. After you've completed one of these workouts, use the worksheet provided to identify the situation you faced, what you'd typically do (usual standard and safety behavior), what you did instead ("good enough" workout), and what happened (outcome). It can also be helpful to take note of how you felt. An example of a completed "good enough" workout worksheet is provided below, as well as a blank worksheet (also available at http://www.newharbinger.com/40064).

| Situation | Usual Standard and Safety Behavior | "Good Enough" Workout (apply "good enough" standard) | Outcome (what happened and how you felt) |
|---|---|---|---|
| Neighbor called to ask if she could pop by and borrow an air pump to fill her bike tires | Clean living room and front hall before she came over | Didn't do any cleaning | Was a little concerned she would notice house wasn't very tidy and be judgmental. Had a quick and pleasant exchange at the door. She didn't really seem to look around. Felt good for helping out. |
| E-mailed a colleague asking a question | Recheck e-mail multiple times for mistakes before sending | Sent without checking | Realized I misspelled something. Colleague never said anything. Sent back e-mail thanking me for getting back to him. Felt embarrassed at first but fine now. |

| Situation | Usual Standard and Safety Behavior | "Good Enough" Workout (apply "good enough" standard) | Outcome (what happened and how you felt) |
|---|---|---|---|
|  |  |  |  |
|  |  |  |  |
|  |  |  |  |
|  |  |  |  |
|  |  |  |  |
|  |  |  |  |

Remember that the more you engage in these workouts, the easier it becomes to apply "good enough" standards to appropriate situations.

Learning when to apply "good enough" standards can be extremely beneficial in daily life. It can save us time and effort, reduce stress, and free up energy to put into other things, such as relationships, recreational activities, and downtime. It also gives us a lot less to worry about!

# In a Nutshell

In this chapter, you learned about a common theme related to problematic worry: perfectionism. Here are some key points:

- Setting high standards and attempting to improve your performance is not the same as being perfectionistic. Perfectionistic expectations tend to be unattainable, costly, and rigid, whereas healthy high standards tend to be attainable, beneficial, and flexible.

- Perfectionistic expectations can be difficult to meet, and our attempts to achieve them can come at a great cost, subsequently contributing to heightened worry and anxiety.

- Perfectionism and intolerance of uncertainty are closely related. Setting excessively high standards and attempting to avoid mistakes can be a way of trying to make outcomes more certain.

- Individuals who hold perfectionistic expectations tend to believe that making mistakes and falling short of perfection will lead to negative outcomes; they therefore use safety behaviors as a means of trying to meet their rigorous standards and make things perfect.

- Behavioral experiments are a way of testing out whether our negative beliefs about perfectionism are actually true. If mistakes and imperfection don't actually lead to catastrophic outcomes that can't be managed, it's important to develop more appropriate expectations considering the cost of perfectionism.

- Different situations call for different standards. Learning when to apply "good enough" standards can be beneficial and cost-effective.

- Developing healthy high standards, and being selective about when to apply those standards, is an important step in further reducing your worry and anxiety.

In this chapter, you learned strategies for managing worries related to perfectionism. In the next chapter, we'll introduce another common worry theme: decision making.

# CHAPTER 7

# Facing the Uncertainty in Decision Making

Making decisions in life can be difficult. This is true regardless of whether you're making big decisions, like deciding on a career or whether to have children, or day-to-day decisions, such as what to make for dinner or what movie to see. Although most people struggle with decision making on occasion, this is particularly true for people who struggle with excessive worry. Research has shown that people who are depressed, anxious, or prone to worry are more likely to be indecisive or to avoid making decisions (Rassin et al. 2007; Rassin and Muris 2005; Spunt, Rassin, and Epstein 2009).

In fact, you might find that even though you worry about different areas of your life—for example, family, relationships, and work—your worries often revolve around the theme of decision making. This next chapter focuses on targeting worries related to making decisions. You'll learn about different types of decisions and decision-making styles, as well as the role intolerance of uncertainty plays in decision making. You'll also have the opportunity to conduct behavioral experiments related to decision making and learn strategies to help you make decisions more confidently and, as a result, worry less.

## The Challenge of Decision Making

What is it about having to make a decision that can be so anxiety-provoking at times? Much of it has to do with the inherent uncertainty present in most decisions: we often can't be sure whether we're making the right decision, whether there's a better decision, or if a chosen decision will lead to a negative outcome. There are many different types of decisions that a person can be faced with, including the following three types, all of which can lead to worry:

1. *Decisions involving preference:* In these situations, you have to make a decision about something that has no clear "right" answer since your choice is ultimately based on personal preference. For example, if Rachel needs to decide what color to paint the walls of her home, there

is really no right choice. The answer will change depending on who is answering it. In fact, if Rachel seeks out reassurance by asking ten different people what color she should pick, she could easily get ten different answers. Moreover, seeking out additional information by researching color combinations online could actually increase the choice of color options, making her decision even more confusing.

2. *Decisions involving missing information:* There are many situations in life where we have to make a decision when information is missing or unavailable to us at the time we're making it. For example, let's say Amy has to decide whether she wants to register for a new course being offered at her school. The difficulty with this decision is that Amy can't predict whether she will like the teacher or the course material since the class is new. She'll therefore have to make a decision based on her best guess about whether she would enjoy the course, without being *sure* it will be a good class.

3. *Decisions with multiple suitable options:* Some of the most difficult decisions we're faced with have multiple suitable options, each with advantages and disadvantages. No matter what decision you make, you'll inherit the disadvantages of your chosen option and lose the advantages of the other options. Let's say that Neville submitted numerous job applications to different companies, both locally and in cities nationwide, and that he received two job offers: one that's local and one that's across the country. The job in another city offers Neville an excellent career opportunity at a good salary, but it is far away from friends and family. The local job does not pay as well, but the staff seems friendly and he would be close to home. Both of these options have pros and cons, such that no matter what he chooses, Neville will have to deal with certain disadvantages. If he takes the local job, he stays close to family and friends and works with people he likes, but he loses the other job's potential for career advancement and better pay. These types of decisions can be particularly anxiety-provoking as they can also involve both preference (for example, differing opinions on the importance of career advancement versus proximity to family and friends) and missing information (since Neville can't know if he'll like the job until after he takes it).

It's important to note that although each of these types of decisions can be anxiety-provoking, not everyone finds decision making challenging. One reason for this is the difference in decision-making styles.

## *What Type of Decision Maker Are You?*

Why is it that some people seem to experience minimal anxiety when faced with decisions and can decide things quickly and efficiently? Research has actually identified two kinds of decision-making styles, and it seems that the type of decision maker you are impacts how you react to decision-making situations. Specifically, people can be either *maximizers* or *satisficers* (Simon 1955, 1956, 1957).

When faced with making a decision, maximizers attempt to find the best possible choice by examining every single option, whereas satisficers search for a "good enough" choice that meets acceptable criteria. For example, let's say you are planning a vacation to Hawaii and you need to pick a hotel for your trip. If you're a maximizer, you might look up all the different hotels in the area and read as many reviews as possible, trying to find the "perfect" accommodations. If, on the other hand, you're a satisficer, you might look up a few hotels and pick the first one that meets your requirements (like a good-quality hotel within a certain price range that is also close to the beach).

Because maximizers want to find the best possible alternative, they typically seek out as many potential options as they can and take longer to make a decision (Dar-Nimrod et al. 2009; Misuraca and Teuscher 2013). Paradoxically, despite putting in more effort to make the best decision, maximizers are often less happy with and more prone to regret their choice, as well as to experience reduced life satisfaction, lower self-esteem, and more depression (Schwartz et al. 2002). Given the strong impact that your approach to decision making has on your well-being and happiness, it's a good idea to identify your own particular decision-making style in the following exercise.

# EXERCISE 7.1:
# Are You a Maximizer or a Satisficer?

The following questionnaire was developed to distinguish between maximizers and satisficers. Read through each statement and rate how much you agree with it, from 1 (completely disagree) to 7 (completely agree).

1. ____ No matter how satisfied I am with my job, it's only right for me to be on the lookout for better opportunities.

2. ____ When I am in the car listening to the radio, I often check other stations to see if something better is playing, even if I am relatively satisfied with what I'm listening to.

3. ____ When I watch TV, I constantly check what's on other channels, even while attempting to watch one program.

4. ____ I treat relationships like clothing: I expect to try a lot on before finding the perfect fit.

5. ____ I often find it difficult to shop for a gift for a friend.

6. ____ Choosing a show or film to watch is really difficult. I'm always struggling to pick the best one.

7. ____ When shopping, I have a hard time finding clothing that I really love.

8. _____ I'm a big fan of lists that attempt to rank things (the best movies, the best singers, the best athletes, the best novels, etc.).

9. _____ I find that writing is very difficult, even if it's just writing an e-mail or text to a friend, because it's so hard to word things just right. I often do several drafts of even simple things.

10. _____ I never settle for second best.

11. _____ Whenever I'm faced with a choice, I try to imagine what all the other possibilities are, even ones that aren't present at the moment.

12. _____ I often fantasize about living in ways that are quite different from my actual life.

13. _____ No matter what I do, I have the highest standards for myself.

Once you've rated each item, add up all your scores and divide that number by 13 to get your average score. If your average is higher than 4, then you're most likely a maximizer. People with average scores greater than 5.5 are considered "extreme maximizers," and those with scores averaging below 2.5 are considered "extreme satisficers" (Schwartz 2004).

---

It's clear that adopting a maximizer decisional style is not helpful in the long run. Yet, if you're someone who worries excessively about decision making, you likely discovered in exercise 7.1 that you're a maximizer. This is because any attempt to find the "perfect" or best solution also serves the goal of reducing uncertainty: if you evaluate every possible option before making a decision, you expect to be more certain that you're picking the best alternative.

However, because it can be impossible to identify every potential option, maximizers are often indecisive and will avoid decision making when possible. In fact, indecisiveness is strongly associated with intolerance of uncertainty and a tendency to view uncertain situations as threatening (Rassin and Muris 2005; Spunt, Rassin, and Epstein 2009). Given this, let's look more directly at the role of intolerance of uncertainty in decision making.

## Uncertainty and Decision Making

When we described the different decision types, you might've noticed that they all involve some uncertainty. This is actually not surprising, since they all involve situations that are either novel, unpredictable, or ambiguous. Amy's decision about whether to register for a new course, for instance, is both a novel and an unpredictable situation, since the class hasn't been offered before and she can't predict whether she will enjoy it. Because of the inherent uncertainty in these types of decisions, people who are intolerant of uncertainty are likely to find decision making threatening.

As discussed in chapter 2, if you're intolerant of the uncertainty in specific situations, then you'll likely have negative beliefs about the uncertainty surrounding those situations. As such, when you have to make a decision but are intolerant of the uncertainty around decision making, you're likely to hold negative beliefs about uncertainty that are specific to decision-making situations. That is, you're likely to believe you'll make a poor decision (the outcome will be negative), that your chosen decision will have very negative consequences (the negative outcome will be catastrophic), and you won't know how to deal with the consequences of the decision (you'll be unable to cope).

As with other situations in which negative beliefs about uncertainty are triggered, you're also likely to worry excessively about any decisions you need to make, experience anxiety, and engage in safety behaviors to cope with the situation. In Amy's case, she might worry, *What if I hate the class? I could end up doing terrible and getting a bad grade that affects my entire GPA! I could try to drop the class before the dropout deadline if I don't like it, but what if I don't realize how difficult the class is until after the deadline?* To cope with these worries, Amy might try to seek reassurance from others, seek out information about the course topic online, read reviews about the teacher, or only partially commit to the course by allowing herself to drop the class if she is at all displeased with it.

## Feared Outcomes in Decision Making

Although the worry cycle for decision-making worries is the same as that for other worry topics, there do tend to be specific feared outcomes and safety behaviors that are most commonly seen with decision making.

Feared outcomes about decision making fall into two categories: (1) concerns about the *chosen decision itself*, and (2) concerns about the *consequences of decision making*. With respect to the decision itself, common fears include making the wrong decision, missing out on a better decision, and not finding the "right" or "perfect" decision. Let's say that Ron is invited to a potluck dinner and decides to bring a carrot cake. He might worry that there was something better he could have made or that there was another dish people would have preferred. In terms of the consequences of decision making, these include worries about the outcome of the "wrong" choice, such as wasting time and effort, feeling personally responsible, and regretting a poor decision. Ron might worry that no one will eat his carrot cake, that he wasted his time making it, or that he'll regret not having made something else the guests would have enjoyed more.

Since the most effective behavioral experiments involve directly testing your beliefs, it's a good idea to identify your specific decision-making fears, which is the intent of the following exercise.

# EXERCISE 7.2:
## Identifying Your Decision-Making Fears

This exercise includes a number of statements about feared outcomes related to decision making. Read over the statements and rate each one according to how typical the statement is of you.

**Scoring:**

1 = Not typical of me

2 = Somewhat typical of me

3 = Very typical of me

\_\_\_\_ I worry that I'll make a bad decision.

\_\_\_\_ I believe that I am bad at making decisions.

\_\_\_\_ I worry that once I make a decision, a better option will come along.

\_\_\_\_ I believe there is a perfect choice when making decisions so long as I think through the decision enough.

\_\_\_\_ I worry that I'll make the wrong decision.

\_\_\_\_ I believe I have to make the best decision possible; otherwise, I will have wasted my time and effort.

\_\_\_\_ I worry that I'll feel bad if I don't make the best or right choice when making decisions.

\_\_\_\_ I worry that I'll regret my decision after I've made it.

\_\_\_\_ I worry that I'll feel personally responsible for any negative outcomes that occur because of my decisions.

\_\_\_\_ I believe that if I make a bad decision, I'll have to cope with lots of negative consequences.

If you scored a 2 or a 3 on any of the above items, then you have likely identified a specific negative belief you have about decision making. Now that you have an idea about your decision-making fears, we can look at your decision-making safety behaviors.

## Safety Behaviors in Decision Making

Safety behaviors for decision-making worries can involve approach or avoidance behaviors, both of which are designed to reduce the uncertainty associated with making decisions. Some common safety behaviors related to decision making include:

*Reassurance seeking:* This can involve asking family and friends for their opinion on what decision you should make or seeking reassurance that you made a good decision.

*Information seeking:* This safety behavior involves gathering a lot of information or doing lots of research before making a decision. For example, before buying a new pair of jeans, you might go to several stores to try on a variety of styles, as well as look up the different prices or reviews of jeans online.

*Avoidance and procrastination:* As with any anxiety-provoking situation, it's common for people who worry about decision making to avoid or put off making decisions. This serves two purposes: first, by avoiding or delaying decision making, you avoid the anxiety that the situation elicits; second, so long as you haven't made a decision, you haven't made the *wrong* decision—that is, there remains the possibility that an as-yet-undiscovered perfect solution could still arise.

*Delegating decisions to others:* Another way to avoid the uncertainty of potentially making a poor decision is to ask others to make decisions for you. In Ron's example, he might ask the host to tell him what he should bring to the potluck.

*Partial commitment:* This safety behavior avoids making an actual decision by attempting to keep your options open—for example, keeping the receipt for a new pair of jeans so you can exchange or return them if you change your mind.

*Impulsive decision making:* Some people cope with indecision by deliberately making a decision "blindly"—that is, making a choice at random rather than thoughtfully making a decision (Barkley-Levenson and Fox 2016). If you're asked to choose which movie to see, for example, you might decide to go to the theater and pick the first movie that's playing when you arrive. Making impulsive decisions is often an attempt to avoid the anxiety and responsibility associated with a potentially bad or wrong decision. In other words, since you didn't give any real thought to your decision, you don't feel personally responsible if the outcome is negative.

*Switching between approach and avoidance:* If you're someone who worries a lot about making decisions, you might find that you often alternate between approach and avoidance safety behaviors. Let's say that Cynthia wants to buy a new mattress. She starts by going to local stores to test out all of the mattresses on display, as well as looking online for sales and reviews of the different types of mattresses (approach safety behavior: information seeking). As the amount of information she obtains grows, Cynthia becomes more anxious about potentially making the wrong decision and thus chooses to delay purchasing a new mattress for the time being (avoidance safety behavior: procrastination). After a few weeks, she goes to look at mattresses in stores again, this time bringing some friends along to help her pick one (approach safety behavior: reassurance seeking). Her friends suggest several different mattresses, but since she's still not completely certain which one would be best for her, she quickly chooses the first mattress her friends liked and speaks to the manager about the store's return policy (avoidance safety behaviors: impulsive decision making and partial commitment). This "dance" between approach and avoidance safety behaviors is often a futile effort to obtain certainty; however, when attempts to completely reduce uncertainty through approach behaviors are unsuccessful, it is common to then switch to avoidance strategies in order to eliminate uncertainty entirely.

Now that you're more familiar with some of the most common safety behaviors associated with decision-making worries, you can identify your own safety behaviors.

## EXERCISE 7.3:
## Identifying Your Decision-Making Safety Behaviors

In this list of common decision-making safety behaviors, place a check next to any category that includes behaviors you engage in when making a decision:

_____ Reassurance seeking (asking others for their advice on decision making or asking for reassurance from others about a decision you already made)

_____ Information seeking (doing research or gathering as much information as possible prior to making a decision)

_____ Avoidance or procrastination (attempts to put off or delay having to make decisions)

_____ Delegating decisions to others (asking others to make decisions for you)

_____ Partial commitment (attempts to make a decision reversible, such as keeping receipts or inquiring about return policies)

_____ Impulsive decision making (deliberate attempts to minimize responsibility for a decision by choosing quickly or at random)

_____ Switching between approach and avoidance behaviors (going back and forth between trying to reduce the uncertainty in decision making and trying to avoid the uncertainty in decision making altogether)

_____  Other decision-making safety behaviors:

_____

_____

_____

If it's difficult to identify your own decision-making safety behaviors, track your worries for a week or two using the worksheet in exercise 3.1 to observe what you actually do when making a decision.

Hopefully, you now have a good idea about both your particular decision-making fears and your safety behaviors when making decisions. Armed with this knowledge, you're in an ideal position to test out the accuracy of your beliefs around decision making.

# Behavioral Experiments Targeting Decision Making

In chapter 3, we discussed that one of the biggest problems with safety behaviors is that they prevent us from finding out whether our negative beliefs are actually correct. This also holds for negative beliefs about decision making. Because of this, it's important to test out the accuracy of your beliefs through behavioral experiments.

As with the experiments described in chapters 4 and 5, the goal here is to deliberately sit with the uncertainty of decision making without engaging in safety behaviors in order to have the opportunity to determine whether your fears are correct. In this case, however, you are testing negative beliefs about the uncertainty of decision making:

*The outcome of decision making will be negative.* This belief assumes that when you make a decision without evaluating every potential option, it will be a poor or wrong choice or you will identify a better option after having made a choice.

*Negative decision-making outcomes will be catastrophic.* This negative belief assumes that you will not only make a bad decision, but that the consequences of that decision will be terrible. For example, you'll feel bad, experience significant regret, or will have wasted lots of time and effort. (You can refer to the beliefs you endorsed in exercise 7.2 to help you identify your own catastrophic fears about decision making.)

*You'll be unable to cope with bad decision making.* This belief assumes that when you do make a poor decision, you'll be overwhelmed by, and unable to deal with, the consequences of that decision.

Because there are different types of decision-making situations, there are also different kinds of behavioral experiments you can conduct to specifically address them. The next sections will describe the various experiments and strategies that can be used to target specific decision-making worries.

## Experiments for Decisions Involving Preference

Because decisions involving preference have no right or perfect answer, it's impossible to attain certainty about one's decision. For example, let's say that Sophie has to decide on a costume for a Halloween party. If she's intolerant of decision-making uncertainty, she might worry that she won't pick the best costume, that no one else will like it, or that there is a better costume she could wear instead. She might then engage in various safety behaviors designed to reduce the uncertainty of making the "wrong" decision, such as spending hours online researching the "perfect" Halloween costume (information seeking), asking someone else to decide for her (delegating responsibility), or not wearing a costume at all (avoidance). In each case, Sophie is attempting to decrease or eliminate her anxiety about making the wrong decision and then having to face her feared consequences of that decision.

With this in mind, behavioral experiments for these types of decisions should "straddle the line" between approach and avoidance safety behaviors. That is, making a decision should involve neither excessive preparation nor impulsivity; rather, it should reflect a thoughtful and efficient decision-making process. In essence, your experiments for these decisions involve acting "as if" you have a satisficer decisional style: you aren't trying to make the perfect decision, you're instead attempting to make the best decision for you at that time. For instance, if you need to buy a new pair of sneakers, a good behavioral experiment would be to go to the shoe store, try on three or four pairs, decide which you like best, and then purchase them immediately.

## Experiments for Decisions Involving Missing Information

Similar to decisions involving preference, there is no perfect or right decision in situations where some information is not available. For example, if you have to choose in January when to take your summer vacation, you can't know for sure what the weather will be like over the summer. It's always possible that it will rain the entire week that you choose to take off. It's this uncertainty that can make these types of decisions so anxiety-provoking, since no amount of planning or research will completely eliminate the uncertainty of the situation.

Common safety behaviors for these kinds of decisions include excessive information seeking, procrastination, impulsive decision making, and partial commitment. Let's say Darryl has two options for a social outing over the weekend: he can go to a friend's dinner party, or he can go to the movies with some family members. Darryl has no way of knowing which activity he'll enjoy more until he actually goes to one of them. He fears that he'll regret his decision if he finds out the other activity would have been better. To cope with this, he might partially commit to both activities by saying that he'll "maybe" attend, then wait until the last minute to quickly decide or ask someone else to decide for him. Or he might try to attend both activities for a short amount of time as a means of avoiding decision making altogether. Although these strategies can reduce anxiety in the moment, they maintain fears associated with decision making.

Behavioral experiments for decisions with missing information involve sitting with the uncertainty of the situation by making decisions that seem best *given the information available at that time.* In other words, when you're faced with these types of decisions, you can thoughtfully review the information available and then choose the option that appears to be the best for you given what you currently know, even though you can't be certain whether your choice is the best option.

## Tips for Developing Useful Decision-Making Experiments

Because there are many different types of fears and safety behaviors associated with decision making, it can be tricky to ensure that you're conducting your behavioral experiments correctly. Here are some guidelines to assist you.

### Use Your Anxiety as a Cue

Behavioral experiments involve deliberately dropping your safety behaviors and inviting uncertainty into your life in order to observe the outcome. You can therefore expect to feel anxious. In fact, feeling anxious lets you know that you're on the right track in terms of a good experiment.

If you find that you aren't anxious at all, you may have inadvertently replaced one safety behavior with another. For example, let's say that your planned experiment involved refraining from excessive information seeking before choosing a restaurant for dinner. If you typically feel the need to research multiple restaurants, checking out all the menus and reviews for each one, this experiment should be anxiety-provoking. If it doesn't cause anxiety, you might have engaged in impulsive decision making instead, just picking the first restaurant you could think of rather than making a thoughtful choice.

### Straddle the Line

An ideal decision-making experiment should always involve a reasoned decision that doesn't involve too much or too little research or information gathering. As discussed earlier, having a satisficer decisional style means that you choose an option that's "good enough" and meets acceptable criteria: although you give thought to your decision, you don't overthink it.

It can be helpful to consider what is most important to you when making certain decisions. Taking the example of a new pair of jeans again, you might decide that a good fit and a reasonable price are most important. You can then complete a behavioral experiment in which you try on two or three pairs and then pick the jeans that fit your criteria best.

## Be Responsible for Your Decisions

A common trap people fall into when making decisions is not maintaining responsibility for their choices. This is usually because we fear being responsible for having made a bad decision. To cope with this, there are a number of safety behaviors we might use, such as partial commitment and impulsive decision making. However, there are also subtle behaviors we can engage in to keep from owning a decision.

For example, let's say Sophie picked a Halloween costume without seeking reassurance or excessive information. Yet she remains concerned that others won't like her costume. As a consequence, she tells people at the party that she's been so busy, she really didn't have time to put together a costume, then apologizes for it not being that great. By letting others know she didn't have the time to make a good decision and apologizing for her perceived bad choice, she is minimizing her responsibility for her decision. But people can't truly own their good decisions and take pride in their successes if they don't allow themselves to take responsibility for potentially bad decisions.

Now that you have an understanding of how to conduct decision-making behavioral experiments, you can begin to test out your own negative beliefs about decision making.

# EXERCISE 7.4:
# Conducting Your Decision-Making Behavioral Experiments

Because there's a great deal of overlap between decisions involving preference and those involving missing information, in this exercise you will develop and carry out behavioral experiments for both decision types.

As a first step, think about daily life decisions you struggle with. These can include decisions that you face regularly (like what to wear to work or what to make for dinner) or decisions that arise on occasion (what clothes to buy or what social outing to attend). Write down some examples of daily decisions that are difficult for you.

## Decision examples:

1. _____

2. _____

3. _____

4. _____

5. _____

Now think about safety behaviors you typically engage in to cope with these decisions. (You can refer to the behaviors you endorsed in exercise 7.3.) With these safety behaviors in mind, write down some behavioral experiments you can conduct for each decision. Don't forget that your experiments should involve deliberately sitting with the uncertainty by refraining from engaging in safety behaviors when making a decision. If you normally ask your spouse what you should make for dinner (delegating responsibility), for example, your experiment could be to choose what meal to make, then prepare it without consulting your spouse beforehand.

## Behavioral experiments you can try:

1. _____

2. _____

3. _____

4. _____

5. _____

Now you can begin conducting your experiments, using the following worksheet to record your findings. Make sure to record your feared outcome(s) before completing the experiment and the actual outcome afterward, as well as how you coped with negative consequences (if any). A sample decision-making experiment is provided, along with a blank worksheet (also available as a PDF at http://www.newharbinger.com/40064).

| Decision-Making Experiment (what you will be doing) | Feared Outcome (what you are worried will happen) | Actual Outcome (what actually happened) | Coping (if the outcome was negative, how you handled it) |
|---|---|---|---|
| Decide on the restaurant where my friends and I will eat—choose three potential restaurants and pick the one I like best (without seeking reassurance). | My friends won't like my choice. They will have a terrible time. I'll regret not having asked my friends where they wanted to eat. I'll be anxious the whole time. | One of my friends is vegan and had a hard time finding something that he could eat from the menu. I had forgotten to check for vegan options. | Spoke to the waiter and we were able to get a vegan dish that my friend could eat. Rest of the evening went well. |
| Decide on a beach day for an upcoming family outing (without information seeking or partial commitment). | What if the weather is bad? What if there was something better I could have chosen to do? I could feel terrible. | It rained the day we planned to go to the beach. | Went to the museum instead and changed plans to go to the beach another day. |

It's a good idea to plan to complete two or three decision-making experiments a week for several weeks. You can come up with new experiments each week or conduct the same one multiple times. For example, if one of your experiments is to limit the time you give yourself to decide what to wear to work (ten minutes instead of thirty to forty), this experiment can be repeated several times.

| Decision-Making Experiment (what you will be doing) | Feared Outcome (what you are worried will happen) | Actual Outcome (what actually happened) | Coping (if the outcome was negative, how you handled it) |
|---|---|---|---|
| | | | |
| | | | |
| | | | |
| | | | |
| | | | |

Because a common fear with decision making is that we'll feel upset or regretful if the outcome is negative, take a moment to think about how you felt after you completed each behavioral experiment. Record any thoughts, feelings, or observations:

_____

_____

_____

---

## Experiments for Decisions Involving Multiple Good Options

In addition to daily life decisions, we sometimes face complex decisions that require thoughtful consideration of the pros and cons of the various choices. When we're particularly anxious about significant decisions, we tend to mentally cycle through the pros and cons of each potential alternative repeatedly without ever reaching a decision. For example, Neville might think, *The local job would be great since I would be close to family, but it wouldn't be so great for my career. Maybe I should take the out-of-town job, since I'll make more money and have an opportunity to advance within the company. But I might be lonely so far from home, and I might not even like the job. Perhaps I should stay here.*

As with most decision-making situations, the absence of a clear "right" answer is a trigger for intolerance of uncertainty. Common safety behaviors as a consequence include reassurance and information seeking, as well as procrastination and avoidance. Particularly when it comes to difficult decisions, we often delay or avoid actually making a decision in the hopes that some unconsidered "perfect" choice might arise. However, if you've given serious thought to a problematic issue, you can assume that if there were a perfect decision to be made, you would have already made it. As such, addressing these situations requires a satisficer decisional style—that is, making a decision that seems good enough based on one's specific criteria instead of trying to find an ideal solution.

For decisions that involve more complex issues, a good strategy is to first identify personally relevant criteria, review the pros and cons of potential options, make a decision, and then follow through with it. So long as you haven't taken action on a decision but instead remain caught in mentally cycling through your options, you're not engaged in productive action. With this in mind, the next exercise will walk you through all the steps of reaching a "good enough" decision when faced with difficult or complex decisions.

# EXERCISE 7.5:
# Managing Complex Decisions

In this exercise (available for download at http://www.newharbinger.com/40064), the goal is to work through and carry out a decision for situations that can be more impactful in our lives. As a first step, write down a few difficult decision-making situations you've been struggling with. (You can refer to your worry tracking sheets from chapters 1 and 3 to help you identify specific problematic situations.)

## Complex or difficult decisions:

Example: *I am not sure whether I should continue staying in my current apartment or move to a new place.*

1. _____

2. _____

3. _____

The next step is to pick one of the situations you listed to work on. Because it's anxiety-provoking to target difficult decision-making situations, choose one that seems the least overwhelming to work on first. As your confidence grows, you can pick more challenging situations. List your chosen situation:

_____

_____

Now that you've picked a situation to work on, think about what criteria are important to you and record them below. You can identify as many criteria as you like, but this doesn't mean that any decision you make will meet all your criteria, so try to come up with a reasonable list and prioritize them from most to least important. Taking the decision of whether or not to move as an example, criteria might include:

1. Size of the apartment: prefer a larger space to live in

2. Location in the city: would like to be close to work

3.   Cost: would like to pay about the same rent as currently

4.   Age of building: would prefer to live in a more modern building (fewer repairs)

# List your own criteria:

Criterion #1: _____

Criterion #2: _____

Criterion #3: _____

Criterion #4: _____

Criterion #5: _____

Criterion #6: _____

Now that you have your list of criteria, write down some of the decision options available to you. Some decisions are either/or situations, but some have more numerous potential options. Remember that you aren't looking for an exhaustive list of choices, but rather a maximum of three or four reasonable options.

Option #1: _____

Option #2: _____

Option #3: _____

Option #4: _____

You can now begin writing down the pros and cons of your options. When you write things down, you can more clearly see the advantages and disadvantages and make a rational choice as a result. In the case of an either/or decision, you can write out the pros and cons for each.

| **Option 1:** *Stay in my current apartment* | **Pros:** <br><br> 1. *Don't have to deal with the hassle of moving* <br><br> 2. *I'm already familiar with the area* <br><br> 3. *I get along with my landlord* | **Cons:** <br><br> 1. *The building is old and needs lots of repairs* <br><br> 2. *The apartment is small* <br><br> 3. *I'm pretty far from work* <br><br> 4. *Walls are thin and it's pretty noisy* |
| --- | --- | --- |
| **Option 2:** *Move to a new apartment* | **Pros:** <br><br> 1. *I could get a place closer to work* <br><br> 2. *I could move into a newer building that doesn't need so many repairs* <br><br> 3. *I could get a bigger place* | **Cons:** <br><br> 1. *Lots of time and effort to move* <br><br> 2. *I have no idea whether I will find a good place* <br><br> 3. *It might be very expensive* <br><br> 4. *Will take time to get used to the neighborhood* |

Using your own decision-making situation, write out your pros and cons for each potential option.

| Option 1: | Pros: | Cons: |
|---|---|---|
| | | |
| Option 2: | Pros: | Cons: |
| | | |
| Option 3: | Pros: | Cons: |
| | | |
| Option 4: | Pros: | Cons: |
| | | |

Only once you write out the advantages and disadvantages of potential choices can you evaluate which option seems to meet most of your criteria. Moreover, although you'll lose some of the pros of other options and inherit the cons of your chosen decision, once you carry out your decision, you can begin to mitigate your losses and potentially recoup some gains.

In the example we've been using, the advantages of moving include the size of the apartment, the location in the city, and the age of the building. By contrast, the main benefits of staying in the same location largely reflect familiarity with the neighborhood and the building. Based on this, the decision that seems to fit the criteria best is to move to a new place.

Looking at your own pros and cons list, identify which potential option seems to best fit your criteria.

**Chosen decision:** _____

As a final step, you need to begin carrying out your decision; otherwise, you're likely to return to worrying about it rather than taking action. You can view this step itself as a behavioral experiment. For example, the next steps in moving to a new place might be to look up rental listings and set up appointments for apartment viewings.

An important difference between behavioral experiments where you sit with uncertainty and the more involved process of complex decision making is the stakes, or importance, of the decision. Deciding to change apartments is a relatively high-stakes situation that warrants more significant consideration, whereas deciding which rental listings to view is not. As such, the latter decision is an ideal behavioral experiment in which to sit with the uncertainty. You might look through the listings, make a quick but thoughtful choice about three or four places to view, and then make appointments for each (without seeking reassurance).

You can also begin to mitigate the potential disadvantages of your chosen decision if appropriate. For example, by setting a price range for rent, you can reduce the likelihood that a new apartment will be too expensive. To ensure that you follow through on your decision, write out the steps involved, as well as a potential time frame in which to complete them.

## Steps for decision-making follow-through:

Step 1: _____

Timeline: _____

Step 2:_____

Timeline: _____

Step 3: _____

Timeline: _____

Step 4: _____

Timeline: _____

Now that you've had some experience making various decisions in the face of uncertainty, you can begin to evaluate the outcome of your experiments.

_____

_____

_____

_____

## Taking Stock of Your Findings

It's important to always review your findings in order to determine if the evidence supports or disputes your negative beliefs about the uncertainty of decision making. By now you should have made a number of decisions without the use of safety behaviors and should therefore be in a position to make some tentative conclusions: How did it go? When you made decisions on a "good enough" principle rather than trying to find the perfect or "right" decision, was there a difference in the results?

We can actually look at these questions along two dimensions: how things actually turned out and how you felt about your decisions:

1. *Decision-making outcomes:* When people start making decisions without the use of safety behaviors, they're often surprised to discover that they're able to make rational decisions quite well. Many outcomes seem to turn out just as well, if not better, when we make decisions based on our own preferences and on what seems best to us at the time. Moreover, even when our choices don't turn out as well as expected, we're often more capable of handling negative outcomes than we thought.

2. *Feelings about decision making:* When we expend a great deal of energy trying to find the perfect option, there's often a great deal of anxiety tied to decision making. Paradoxically, although embracing some of the uncertainty around decision making can be more anxiety-provoking at first, people often report feeling happier with their choices overall and less likely to experience regret about their decisions (Schwartz et al. 2002). Specifically, adopting a satisficer ("good enough") decisional style seems to lead to greater satisfaction overall with chosen decisions.

# EXERCISE 7.6:
## Evaluating Your Decision Making

This exercise is best completed once you have a number of decision-making experiments under your belt. In this manner, you can begin to get a more accurate picture of your actual decision-making ability without the use of safety behaviors, as well as evaluate the accuracy of your negative beliefs about uncertainty in decision making. You can also evaluate your feelings both during and after the decision-making process.

Using your findings from the experiments you conducted in exercises 7.4 and 7.5, answer the following questions (you can also print out this questionnaire for future use at http://www.newharbinger.com /40064):

How many decision-making experiments did you do? _____

How many turned out positive (that is, you were satisfied with the outcome)? _____

How many turned out negative (you were unhappy with the outcome)? _____

How often was a negative outcome catastrophic? _____

_____

When the outcome was negative, how often were you able to handle the situation?

_____

_____

How often did you handle the situation well (you were satisfied with your coping)?

_____

_____

Overall, do you think you did well in making your own decisions?

_____

_____

How often did you feel anxious when making decisions while uncertain? _____

_____

_____

If you did feel anxious, did that feeling lessen as you made more decisions? _____

_____

_____

How often did you regret your decisions after you made them? _____

_____

_____

Thinking back to how you made decisions in the past, did you feel more or less regretful of your decisions when you engaged in safety behaviors during decision making?

_____

_____

Overall, what do you think of your feelings when making decisions without safety behaviors?

_____

_____

_____

Remember that we're most likely to change our beliefs when there is lots of compelling evidence to do so. It's therefore a good idea to refer back to this exercise periodically to continue to develop a complete and accurate picture of your decision-making outcomes and feelings.

# Becoming a Good Decision Maker

This chapter focused on addressing your worries about making decisions across all areas of your life. One of the best ways to reduce worry about decision making is to become more confident in your decision-making ability. This is accomplished in two ways: First, by allowing yourself to make decisions without the use of exhaustive strategies to avoid or eliminate uncertainty, you get to see how capable you are of making decisions when you rely only on your own preferences and your rational thinking skills. Second, we're more confident in our abilities when we think we're good at something.

Expertise in any skill is something we develop through practice. So the more you do something, the more confident you are in your ability to do it. A good example is when we learn how to drive. The more often you drive, the more you develop and refine your driving skills and, as a result, the more confident you become. The same applies to decision making. In essence, *good decision makers are people who make decisions.*

Another key element to becoming a good decision maker is recognizing when a situation requires a great deal of thought and when it doesn't. For example, although it's a good idea to really think through the decision of whether to buy a house, it should be relatively simple to decide what to make for dinner. When we worry excessively about making decisions, even simple decisions, like deciding on a dinner menu, can become anxiety-provoking and lead to behaviors such as looking up every recipe possible and asking for excessive reassurance from family members about what would be best to make.

However, research has shown that the more effort we put into a task, the more value we give to that task (Aronson and Mills 1959). This means that if you put a lot of effort into even minor decisions, the importance of whatever you decide will be inflated: it will "feel" like a big deal even when it isn't. As such, although we recommend that you take the time to thoughtfully work through the decision-making process for important decisions (as described in exercise 7.5), smaller daily life decisions can be resolved relatively quickly.

# In a Nutshell

In this chapter, we focused on worries related to the theme of decision making. As with other worries described in this workbook, the main target is not the worries themselves, but rather the negative beliefs about the uncertainty surrounding decision making that fuels worries about decisions in the first place. Here are some key points:

- Decisions most likely to lead to worry and anxiety typically involve personal preference, missing information, and multiple plausible options. All of these types of decisions are uncertain, so there's no way to know whether we're making the right or perfect decision.

- There are two decision-making styles: (1) maximizers try to find the best possible option when making decisions by examining every choice; (2) satisficers try to make "good enough" decisions by making a choice based on limited options that meet acceptable criteria.

- Although maximizers try to find every available option in order to make the best possible decision, they're typically less happy with the results of their decisions and more prone to regret their decisions.

- People who struggle with making decisions are likely to hold negative beliefs about the uncertainty surrounding decision-making situations. That is, you're likely to believe that you'll make poor decisions and that the consequences of such decisions will be negative. Consequently, you're likely to engage in safety behaviors as a means of preventing those negative outcomes from occurring.

- When conducting behavioral experiments on daily life decisions, remember to straddle the line between seeking too much and too little information, and to take responsibility for your decisions, since owning your occasional failures means you also get to own your successes.

- The best way to reduce your worries about decision making is to increase your confidence in your ability to make decisions. This is accomplished by actually making decisions free from safety behaviors. The more decisions you make, the more confident you'll become.

- Put forth only as much effort into making a decision as the situation requires. Simple daily life decisions should be resolved quickly, with the goal of finding a "good enough" option.

Over the past two chapters, we've introduced two common themes seen across worry topics—perfectionism and decision making—as well as specific strategies to address each theme. We will now turn our attention to worries present across various anxiety disorders and how targeting the fear of uncertainty in this context continues to play an important role in worry management.

CHAPTER 8

# Facing the Uncertainty
# in Anxiety Disorders

Worry and anxiety exist on a continuum. Some people experience only occasional mild levels, while others experience more severe and frequent episodes. In mental health, a line is drawn on this continuum, identifying worry and anxiety as a potential problem, or "disorder," when they're experienced as intense and frequent, causing significant distress and interference in daily functioning (APA 2013). It's important to realize, however, that this distinction is often a matter of degree. That is, people on the anxiety disorder side of the line are not fundamentally different than those without an anxiety disorder; rather, the worry and anxiety they experience are more severe and their symptoms lead to greater impairment.

Up until now, the strategies presented in this workbook have been aimed at helping anyone who experiences problematic worry, regardless of what they worry about or how much they worry. But in this chapter, we focus specifically on strategies for individuals who have been diagnosed with, or believe that they might have, an anxiety or anxiety-related disorder. These strategies are tailored to the unique aspects of particular anxiety problems, providing the additional tools needed to successfully reduce worry and anxiety.

## Uncertainty in Anxiety Disorders

There are different types of anxiety or anxiety-related disorders, and they're differentiated by the particular "threat" that leads to the anxiety. It's this particular threat, or fear, that helps us discriminate among the various anxiety disorders, not the anxiety itself, because anxiety "feels" like anxiety no matter what triggers it. To illustrate, the threat that triggers people with social anxiety disorder (SAD) is potentially saying or doing something embarrassing that might lead others to judge them negatively. This threat leads to worry about social situations, which in turn leads to anxiety. Alternatively, someone who struggles with illness anxiety disorder (IAD) is triggered by unexplained physical symptoms, which lead to worries about potentially having a serious illness or disease. In each case, the individual experiences worry and anxiety, but what triggers those feelings is different depending on the anxiety disorder.

Given that anxiety disorders involve different types of threats, we need to target slightly different things when managing them. Yet despite the wide range of different threat triggers, and the anxiety disorders they can lead to, research suggests that they all share a common feature: intolerance of uncertainty.

As discussed in chapter 2, intolerance of uncertainty stems from a set of negative beliefs about uncertainty. Research shows that intolerance of uncertainty is related to various anxiety and anxiety-related disorders (Boelen and Carleton 2012; Carleton, Collimore, and Asmundson 2010; Carleton et al. 2014; Carleton et al. 2012; Counsell et al. 2017; Fergus and Valentiner 2011; Gentes and Ruscio 2011; Ladouceur et al. 1999; Oglesby et al. 2016). However, research also suggests that there is disorder-specific intolerance of uncertainty (Shihata, McEvoy, and Mullan 2016; Thibodeau et al. 2015). That is, individuals diagnosed with different anxiety disorders hold negative beliefs about the specific uncertainties related to their specific disorder. For example, someone who has generalized anxiety disorder (GAD) has negative beliefs around the uncertainties involving everyday activities, while someone with obsessive-compulsive disorder (OCD) characterized by contamination obsessions, for example, holds negative beliefs around the uncertainties related to the dangers of coming into contact with bodily fluids. This means that it's important not only to address intolerance of uncertainty in general, but also to target disorder-specific intolerance of uncertainty as a means of managing worry.

Just as we saw with worries involving decision making and perfectionism, there are disorder-specific safety behaviors related to various anxiety disorders, and research has shown that safety behaviors play a role in maintaining those disorders (Blakey and Abramowitz 2016; Helbig-Lang and Petermann 2010; Salkovskis 1991). An essential key to overcoming worry is conducting behavioral experiments that deliberately drop safety behaviors, since such experiments allow us to directly test out the accuracy of our beliefs about the threat of uncertainty. The same holds true for anxiety disorders: research shows that behavioral experiments are an effective strategy in treating anxiety and anxiety-related disorders (McMillan and Lee 2010).

Throughout the remainder of this chapter, we will highlight four different disorders that all involve significant worry and have been linked to the fear of uncertainty: generalized anxiety disorder, social anxiety disorder, obsessive-compulsive disorder, and illness anxiety disorder. If you've already been diagnosed with an anxiety disorder, you can proceed to the section relevant to you. But if you haven't been diagnosed with an anxiety disorder and think that one (or more) applies to you—or you just aren't sure—we encourage you to check out all the sections.

# Generalized Anxiety Disorder

Generalized anxiety disorder involves excessive and uncontrollable worry about any number of daily life events (such as getting to places on time, getting tasks done at work, having enough money for retirement; APA 2013). Although it's normal to experience heightened worry and anxiety during times of stress, the worry related to GAD is excessive because it's more than would be expected given the situation (for example, worrying about a loved one's health even when they're not sick) and it's experienced as uncontrollable. In essence, people with GAD worry about the same things that everyone else does, but their worry is more frequent, excessive given the situation, and difficult to control.

GAD worry is also chronic (experienced more days than not for at least six months), with many people reporting that they can't remember a time when they didn't worry. Individuals diagnosed with GAD also experience physical symptoms, including feelings of restlessness, fatigue, difficulty concentrating, irritability, muscle tension, and sleep problems.

## GAD and the General Fear of Uncertainty

Although people with GAD worry about several different things (work/school, family, interpersonal relationships, health, finances, minor matters), their worries are likely triggered by the uncertainty in daily life situations. Individuals with GAD hold negative beliefs about the *general* state of uncertainty, and as a result, they experience worry related to most anything (Robichaud and Dugas 2015). For example, no one can be completely certain how things will go in a meeting, if their kids will be safe while on a field trip, or if their partner's health will deteriorate. As a consequence, if you're someone who is threatened by the uncertainty in daily life situations, there's always something to worry about, simply because life is inherently uncertain. What people with GAD worry about can change from day to day depending on what uncertain situations they face at any given time, and it's this general intolerance of uncertainty that fuels the engine of worry in GAD.

## GAD-Specific Safety Behaviors

GAD safety behaviors involve actions designed to avoid or minimize exposure to uncertainty as much as possible. They include both *approach* behaviors, which aim to reduce or eliminate the uncertainty in a given situation (for example, excessive reassurance seeking or information seeking), and *avoidant* behaviors, which are designed to cope with uncertainty by avoiding an uncertain situation altogether (for example, procrastination or delegating tasks to others). Identifying the GAD safety behaviors you engage in is an important step in constructing GAD behavioral experiments.

# EXERCISE 8.1:
# Identifying Your Specific GAD Safety Behaviors

Read over the list of safety behaviors related to GAD below and place a check next to each one you've used to cope with daily life worries. (You can flip back to exercise 3.2 for a full description of the safety behavior categories.)

Note: When reviewing all of the safety behavior checklists in this chapter, keep in mind that safety behaviors are considered problematic only if they're performed in an attempt to reduce anxiety and prevent feared outcomes. Safety behaviors are not inherently bad or unhelpful. If you engage in an action such as delegating a task to others because it's something you prefer not to do or you're too busy, and not because you're anxious to do it yourself, then this isn't a safety behavior. As such, check only the items that represent safety behaviors you typically use to address uncertainty in feared situations.

## Safety Behaviors

_____ Avoidance

_____ Procrastination

_____ Impulsive decision making

_____ Partial commitment

_____ Delegating responsibility to others

_____ Doing everything yourself (not delegating tasks)

_____ Excessive reassurance seeking

_____ Checking

_____ Excessive information seeking

_____ Excessive preparation

What other GAD-related safety behaviors do you engage in?

_____

With this information in hand, you're ready to start identifying specific behavioral experiments.

## GAD Behavioral Experiments

Conducting behavioral experiments related to GAD involves testing the accuracy of your beliefs about the threat of uncertainty in general. When you complete a GAD behavioral experiment, you're making a prediction about the outcome of an uncertain situation and then deliberately facing that situation without using your typical safety behaviors. For instance, if you typically avoid driving to unfamiliar places because you're afraid you'll get lost, a good experiment would be to drive to a new area of town and observe what actually happens. If you normally research various routes and leave early when driving to an unfamiliar area, your experiment might involve doing a quick map search and not leaving too early.

The good news is that if you've been working through this workbook chapter by chapter, you've already been targeting your daily life worries through behavioral experiments. The goal now is to conduct additional behavioral experiments related to your various worry themes in order to make sure you're adequately testing out your beliefs about uncertainty.

# EXERCISE 8.2:
# Constructing GAD Behavioral Experiments

Because worry topics in GAD can include any type of uncertain situation, there are many different types of experiments you can conduct. Go through the themed lists below and next to each potential experiment, write down the level of anxiety (from 0 to 10, with 0 = no anxiety and 10 = severe anxiety) you would expect to feel if faced with that situation. (Refer back to exercise 4.1 for additional ideas for experiments.)

### Experiments Targeting Danger/Safety

_____ Go for a walk by yourself in your neighborhood

_____ Go for a walk by yourself in a less familiar residential neighborhood or busy downtown area

_____ Stay home alone for a night

_____ Go out without your cell phone

_____ Leave your earthquake or car safety kit at home when going out for a day trip

_____ Let your kids play on the playground

What other experiments targeting danger/safety can you think of?

_____

_____

## Experiments Targeting Work/School

\_\_\_\_ Don't recheck a work-related e-mail

\_\_\_\_ Complete a work or school assignment without rechecking it before handing it in

\_\_\_\_ Hand in work or school assignments without seeking reassurance from others

\_\_\_\_ Delegate a work task to a colleague

\_\_\_\_ Complete a task even if you're not 100 percent certain you know how to do it

What other experiments targeting work/school can you think of?

_____

_____

## Experiments Targeting Interpersonal Relationships

\_\_\_\_ Don't phone or text your family members while they're out

\_\_\_\_ Make firm plans with a friend or family member for the weekend despite not knowing if you'll be up for it

\_\_\_\_ Text a family member without rechecking it

\_\_\_\_ Phone a friend you've been avoiding

What other experiments targeting interpersonal relationships can you think of?

_____

_____

### Experiments Targeting Daily Activities and Responsibilities

\_\_\_\_ Don't plan your route ahead of time to an unfamiliar location

\_\_\_\_ Don't leave early for a social event

\_\_\_\_ Try a new class (yoga, cooking)

\_\_\_\_ Make a minor decision about buying something without doing any research

\_\_\_\_ Delegate a responsibility to a family member (getting groceries, paying a bill)

\_\_\_\_ Leave the house without double-checking that the door is locked (or check only once)

\_\_\_\_ Leave the dishwasher or laundry dryer going when out running an errand

What other experiments targeting daily activities and responsibilities can you think of?

_____

_____

Now that you have some ideas of behavioral experiments that are relevant to you, you're ready to start planning and conducting them. Turn to exercise 8.9 to get started.

# Social Anxiety Disorder

Social anxiety disorder involves excessive fear and anxiety when interacting with others or when in situations where one might be observed or evaluated by others (APA 2013). Although it's normal to experience anxiety in social situations on occasion, individuals with SAD constantly feel "on stage" and are overly concerned that they'll do something embarrassing or humiliating (for example, *I'll say something stupid* or *I'll look anxious*) or that others will think badly of them (*They'll think I'm stupid or weird* or *They won't like me*). As a result, they tend to avoid social situations or endure them with great distress.

SAD can impact all facets of life and can interfere with daily tasks (such as our ability to run errands, go grocery shopping), with work or school (such as our ability to attend and participate in classes and meetings, to talk to classmates and colleagues), and with our social lives (such as our ability to participate in social outings, to develop and maintain friendships).

## Social Anxiety and the Uncertainty of Social Situations

Social situations are inherently uncertain. When interacting with others, we can never be entirely certain how it'll go. We can't be sure that we're presenting ourselves the way we want, and we don't know for certain how others will behave or react to us. And since no one can read minds, we can't be sure exactly what others are thinking about us or whether they're enjoying the interaction.

In addition, we're constantly sending one another "messages" through either verbal or nonverbal cues or behaviors. For example, when we smile and make eye contact with someone, we're often sending them the message that we're friendly and interested in engaging with them. But we really can't be 100 percent certain what other people's behaviors actually mean. If you're out for lunch with a friend who's constantly checking her watch, you can't be sure whether she's sending you the message that she's bored or whether she actually has an appointment to get to and is just cueing you that she may need to leave soon.

Individuals with SAD hold negative beliefs about the uncertainty related to social situations, and they tend to fear outcomes related to embarrassing themselves and others thinking badly of them.

## SAD-Specific Safety Behaviors

There are a variety of safety behaviors related to social anxiety disorder (Clark et al. 1995), and they can be grouped into two categories (Hirsch, Meynen, and Clark 2004; Plasencia, Alden, and Taylor 2011). The first is *avoidance behaviors,* which include actions aimed at reducing one's involvement in a social situation (such as averting eye contact or sitting on the edge of groups). The second is *impression management,* which includes behaviors intended to control one's impression on others (such as being overly agreeable or rehearsing what you say before you say it). Identifying SAD safety behaviors that you use is an important step in constructing relevant behavioral experiments.

## EXERCISE 8.3:
## Identifying Your Specific Social Anxiety Safety Behaviors

Review the lists of SAD-related safety behaviors below and check all of the behaviors you use in an attempt to reduce the uncertainty in social situations.

### Avoidance Behaviors

_____ Limiting social interactions or avoiding them altogether

_____ Avoiding or making minimal eye contact

_____ Saying very little

_____ Censoring what you say

_____ Cutting conversations short

_____ Avoiding sharing opinions and ideas

_____ Appearing distant or busy

_____ Avoiding talking about yourself or sharing personal information

_____ Sitting on the outside of groups or trying to position yourself so as not to be noticed

What are other avoidance-related safety behaviors you engage in?

_____

## Impression Management

_____ Making an effort to get your words just right

_____ Rehearsing what you're going to say before you say it

_____ Preparing topics of discussion ahead of time

_____ Acting overly agreeable

_____ Excessively planning for social situations

_____ Deliberately talking a lot

_____ Trying to avoid pauses while speaking

_____ Trying to conceal your anxiety (for example, wearing a turtleneck to hide signs of blushing, gripping a cup to avoid hands shaking)

What are other impression management safety behaviors you engage in?

_____

With this information in hand, you're ready to start identifying specific behavioral experiments.

## *SAD-Specific Behavioral Experiments*

Conducting behavioral experiments related to SAD involves testing the accuracy of your beliefs about the threat of uncertainty in social situations by taking a small social risk and facing the situation without using your typical safety behaviors. This allows you to observe what actually happens in uncertain social situations, as well as your ability to cope with negative outcomes if and when they occur. For example, if you normally avoid phoning friends because you're worried that they won't want to talk to you, a good behavioral experiment might be to phone a friend and then observe the outcome. Or if you normally plan your conversations ahead of time because you're worried you'll say something stupid, you might decide to have a brief and unplanned conversation with a friend instead. In both cases, you're taking a social risk because you aren't completely sure what will happen in these social situations.

When developing your SAD behavioral experiments, give some thought to what your feared outcome would look like. Specifically, if you anticipate that a social interaction will go poorly when you don't engage in safety behaviors, think about how you would actually *know* that the interaction did not go well: did the person look away, roll their eyes, cut the conversation short, or otherwise look uninterested? Perhaps you expect that you wouldn't initially know whether it went well, since the person might be polite at first. In this case, you might predict that the person would avoid you or not answer your calls or texts later on.

Because we can easily make the mistake of assuming that a social interaction did not go well without any real evidence, it's important to have a clear idea beforehand about what your feared outcome would look like. Make sure your feared social outcome involves an observable outcome that allows for accurate testing of your beliefs. Remember that behavioral experiments are expected to cause some anxiety, so feeling anxious or uncomfortable is not evidence that the social interaction was negative.

---

# EXERCISE 8.4:
# Constructing SAD Behavioral Experiments

To plan your own SAD behavioral experiments, go through the list below of different types of experiments targeting the uncertainty in social situations. Next to each potential experiment, write down the level of anxiety (from 0 to 10) you would expect to feel if you faced that situation.

### Experiments Targeting Social Situations

\_\_\_\_\_  Walk around alone in public (grocery store, busy mall)

\_\_\_\_\_  Start a conversation with a cashier or barista (ask a question, make an observation)

_____ Approach a stranger and ask for help (ask what time it is, ask for directions)

_____ Accept an invitation to a social outing or gathering, then attend

_____ Start a conversation with a classmate or work colleague

_____ Ask or answer a question in a class or meeting

_____ Present in a meeting or in a class

_____ Return an item you purchased to a store

_____ Phone a store to ask a question (hours of operations, if they have something in stock)

_____ Phone or text a friend

_____ Express an opinion (about a movie or restaurant)

_____ Tell a story to a group of people

_____ Make a toast (at a dinner party or celebration)

_____ Say no to an unreasonable demand (without excessively apologizing or providing excessive explanations)

_____ Eat or drink in public

_____ Use a public washroom while other people are in the room

_____ Draw attention to yourself (speak loudly in a coffee shop or store)

_____ Make a mistake, such as mispronouncing a word, when interacting with others

(Chapter 6 also contains lots of great ideas on making mistakes and being imperfect in social situations.)

What are some other behavioral experiments related to SAD that you can think of?

_____

_____

Now that you have some ideas of behavioral experiments that are relevant to you, you're ready to start planning and conducting them. Turn to exercise 8.9 to get started.

# Obsessive-Compulsive Disorder

Obsessive-compulsive disorder includes the presence of obsessions and compulsions (APA 2013). Obsessions are repetitive, intrusive, and unwanted thoughts (for example, thoughts of accidentally harming someone, being contaminated by germs) that cause a great deal of distress and anxiety. Compulsions, on the other hand, are repetitive behaviors (such as washing, checking, arranging) or mental acts (counting, repeating phrases, praying) that people deliberately engage in as an attempt to reduce the anxiety related to their obsessions and to prevent feared outcomes from occurring. For example, if you have obsessions about being exposed to dangerous germs after you've touched a door-knob (contamination obsession), you might engage in excessive hand washing (compulsion) in order to feel less anxious and prevent yourself from becoming ill.

Although it's common for people to describe themselves as "OCD" if they engage in specific behaviors such as frequent hand washing, double-checking locks, and preferring things to be arranged, organized, or cleaned in a specific way, a diagnosis of OCD is warranted only if the obsessions and compulsions are time-consuming and cause significant distress and interference in your daily life.

## OCD and the Uncertainty of Danger

There are numerous presentations of OCD, and individuals can experience obsessions with different themes and engage in a variety of compulsions. However, in this section, we'll focus specifically on obsessions and compulsions related to doubt, accidental harm to others, and contamination. Central to these obsessional themes are the uncertainty around safety and the potential for danger.

*Obsessions related to doubt* involve fears about the uncertainty of not having done something properly or having made a mistake, such as, *Am I sure I locked the door and turned the stove off?* or *Am I sure I answered that text correctly?* People who experience these obsessions often worry about the consequences of being unsure: *What if I didn't lock the door and someone breaks into the house?* or *What if I didn't express myself properly in the text and now my friend is angry with me?*

*Obsessions related to harm to others* involve fears about the uncertainty of accidentally causing harm to others through carelessness, including, *Am I sure I didn't hit someone when driving?* or *Am I sure I took appropriate care when cooking the chicken so that I didn't accidentally make my family sick?*

*Obsessions related to contamination* involve fears about the uncertainty of being exposed to dirt, germs, chemicals, or bodily fluids. People who experience these types of obsessions tend to worry about the potential danger resulting from exposure to contaminants. Examples include, *What if I develop HIV from using public bathrooms?* and *Am I sure I got all the cleaning fluid off my hands after I washed the sink?*

Although obsessions are a core component of OCD, they share a common feature with worry: the fear of uncertainty. As such, it should come as no surprise that people with OCD engage in safety behaviors, which include various compulsions aimed at reducing or eliminating the uncertainty regarding their obsessions. The problem is that it's always *possible* that something bad could happen, even if it's very unlikely: it's possible that you'll forget to lock the front door and your house will be robbed, that despite being a cautious driver you could still hit a pedestrian, that touching a doorknob could expose you to germs that make you sick. But trying to be completely certain about every potential danger is exhausting, and it may not be necessary, especially if we're overestimating the actual level of danger.

## OCD-Specific Safety Behaviors

Because compulsions in OCD function in the same way that safety behaviors do—that is, they reduce anxiety in the short term and are designed to prevent feared outcomes—we will refer to OCD compulsions as "safety behaviors" throughout this section. As we've seen with other anxiety disorders, individuals with OCD engage in various approach behaviors (seeking reassurance, checking, excessive washing or cleaning) and avoidance behaviors (avoiding touching things, delegating tasks to others) that interfere with the ability to test out the accuracy of beliefs about uncertainty.

Interestingly, research on OCD-related compulsions shows that engaging in safety behaviors like checking results in greater self-doubt and leads to increased checking behavior (Linkovski et al. 2016; Radomsky, Gilchrist, and Dussault 2006; Radomsky and Alcolado 2010). In the case of OCD, the search for certainty not only maintains OCD, but increases the frequency of symptoms.

---

## EXERCISE 8.5:
## Identifying Your Specific OCD Safety Behaviors

Review the lists of safety behaviors related to OCD and check all that you engage in.

### Safety Behaviors Related to Doubt

\_\_\_\_\_ Repeatedly checking that doors (house or car) are locked

\_\_\_\_\_ Repeatedly checking windows (to ensure they are properly closed and/or locked)

\_\_\_\_\_ Repeatedly checking that appliances are off (stove, iron, coffeemaker)

\_\_\_\_\_ Seeking reassurance from others that doors are locked and appliances are off

\_\_\_\_\_ Unplugging appliances (toaster, coffeemaker)

_____ Redoing or reviewing things to make sure you did them properly (for example, rechecking that you properly filled out a form or answered an e-mail/text appropriately)

_____ Creating a "memory trick" to reduce doubt (like turning off appliances at home in a particular order and describing out loud what you're doing while doing it)

## Safety Behaviors Related to Harm to Others

_____ Avoiding (for example, avoiding driving places where there are lots of pedestrians in case you hit one or avoiding preparing food in case you accidentally poison others)

_____ Engaging in excessive cautiousness (such as driving very slowly past pedestrians to make sure you don't hit anyone or excessively cleaning while cooking in order to ensure that food is safely prepared)

_____ Repeatedly checking (for instance, checking in with family members to make sure they're safe or checking that you didn't harm anyone when driving by retracing your route)

_____ Seeking reassurance that you didn't do anything that could harm others

_____ Delegating tasks to others (asking others to prepare meals or to drive)

## Safety Behaviors Related to Contamination

_____ Avoiding touching or coming into contact with various contaminants (like household cleaners, pets, garbage)

_____ Avoiding touching things in public places (doorknobs, elevator buttons)

_____ Avoiding using public restrooms

_____ Using your sleeve or tissue to open doors or turn on faucets

_____ Excessive or ritualized hand washing

_____ Excessive or ritualized showering

_____ Excessive or ritualized cleaning

_____ Seeking reassurance related to contamination concerns

_____ Not allowing items worn outside (clothes, shoes) into your home

_____ Researching information related to contamination

What are some other safety behaviors related to OCD that you can think of?

_____

With this information in hand, you're ready to start identifying behavioral experiments targeting OCD.

## OCD-Specific Behavioral Experiments

Conducting OCD behavioral experiments involves once again testing the accuracy of beliefs about the danger related to uncertainty. When you complete an OCD experiment, you're making a prediction about the danger related to an uncertain situation and then deliberately facing that situation without using your typical safety behaviors or compulsions. For example, if you normally avoid driving in areas where there are lots of pedestrians because you're afraid you might hit someone, a good behavioral experiment would be to drive in a busier neighborhood and observe whether your prediction is correct.

# EXERCISE 8.6:
## Constructing OCD Behavioral Experiments

To plan your own OCD behavioral experiments, go through the lists below of different types of experiments. Next to each potential experiment, write down the level of anxiety (from 0 to 10) you would expect to feel in that situation.

### Experiments Related to Doubt

_____ Leave the house without checking that the door is locked (or check only once)

_____ Go to bed without checking that the doors are locked (or check only once)

_____ Park your car in a parking lot and go shopping without checking the car door locks (or check them only once)

_____ Leave the house without checking to make sure all the appliances are off (or check only once)

_____ Leave the house without unplugging appliances (coffeemaker and toaster)

_____ Leave the house with an appliance running (laundry dryer or dishwasher)

_____ Don't seek reassurance from others that you did lock doors and turn off appliances

_____ Don't check with others to ensure that they locked doors and turned off appliances

_____ Fill out forms or send e-mails/texts without rechecking that you did it correctly

What are some other behavioral experiments related to doubt that you can think of?

_____

_____

## Experiments Related to Harm to Others

_____ Drive past cyclists (without looking into your rearview mirror or retracing your route to make sure you didn't hit them)

_____ Drive in an area with lots of pedestrians (without looking in your rearview mirror afterward and without retracing your route to check on the safety of the pedestrians)

_____ Go for a drive and avoid inspecting your vehicle for damage (of having hit someone) after returning home

_____ Prepare food for others without seeking reassurance that you prepared things properly

_____ Prepare food for others without checking to see if they're okay after they eat

_____ Prepare food for others without excessively cleaning surfaces or removing potential contaminants (leave dish detergent on counter)

_____ Let children engage in activities that have a low probability of harm (playing at the park, jumping on a netted trampoline)

What are some other behavioral experiments related to harm to others that you can think of?

_____

_____

**Experiments Related to Contamination**

_____ Touch something "contaminated" (garbage bin, sticky surface, household cleaners) and only wash your hands for two minutes _____ (or one minute _____; twenty seconds _____)

_____ Touch doorknobs and elevator buttons in public places (then do not wash your hands for a minimum of thirty minutes afterward)

_____ Use public washrooms

_____ Walk around public places where there are possible contaminants (the mall, an alley, around garbage bins)

_____ Go out to public places and don't change your clothes when you get home

_____ Wear shoes you wore outside inside your home

What are some other behavioral experiments related to contamination that you can think of?

_____

_____

Now that you have some ideas of behavioral experiments that are relevant to you, you're ready to start planning and conducting them. Turn to exercise 8.9 to get started.

# Illness Anxiety Disorder

Illness anxiety disorder, also referred to as "health anxiety," involves an excessive preoccupation with having or developing a serious illness or disease, as well as increased anxiety around changes in health status or bodily symptoms (APA 2013). People with health anxiety become extremely anxious when noticing even a minor physical symptom, such as a skipped heartbeat or general aches and pains.

It's completely normal to be concerned about your health on occasion, particularly if you're struggling with a specific health problem or if there is a family history of a specific condition (such as heart disease), but the health worries of people with IAD are excessive and disproportionate to the situation. If you have health-related worries, you might be concerned about developing one particular disease or illness (cancer, Parkinson's disease), or you might worry about different health problems depending on the physical symptom you're experiencing at the time (concern about having stomach cancer due to stomach pain).

Although people with IAD will often receive medical tests related to their feared health issues (a scan to assess for tumors or an ECG to assess for a heart condition), they are typically not reassured when the results indicate that there is no physical problem.

## IAD and the Uncertainty of Bodily Changes

Our bodies are constantly changing. We all experience unexplained bodily symptoms occasionally, including minor aches and pains, unusual sensations (such as dizziness or nausea), and changes in functioning (such as reduced energy levels). Research suggests that in 25 to 50 percent of primary care medical visits, no cause is identified for the physical symptoms experienced by patients (Barsky and Borus 1995). Most often, these physical symptoms are either normal bodily changes that pass on their own or something benign and/or easily treatable (Verhaak et al. 2006).

There is inherent uncertainty around our health and what bodily changes mean. Developing a good relationship with your health involves learning to live with the uncertainty of unexpected physical sensations without being overly focused on minor changes or overly avoidant and in denial about serious problems.

## IAD-Specific Safety Behaviors

To cope with health-related worries, individuals with IAD often engage in approach behaviors designed to reduce the uncertainty of unexplained or unexpected physical sensations, including excessive help-seeking behaviors like frequent doctor visits, online medical searches, and repeated checking of one's body for signs of illness. Alternatively, some people engage in avoidant safety behaviors, such as avoiding regular doctor checkups and avoiding conversations, movies, or news articles dealing with health-related issues. Although these behaviors (such as seeking reassurance from doctors) can make us feel better in the short term, they're related to increased anxiety in the long term, as well as increased reassurance-seeking behaviors in the future (Salkovskis and Warwick 1986).

## EXERCISE 8.7:
## Identifying Your Specific Health Anxiety Safety Behaviors

Review the lists of IAD-related safety behaviors below and check all that you engage in.

## Approach Safety Behaviors

_____ Checking body for signs of illness (probing for lumps, assessing moles, monitoring pain)

_____ Monitoring vitals (blood pressure, pulse)

_____ Seeking reassurance from friends and family about symptoms

_____ Excessive researching (usually online) of signs and symptoms of various illnesses and diseases

_____ Going for frequent doctor visits

_____ Always carrying a cell phone with you in case of a medical emergency

_____ Always having food and water, as well as medication, with you in case you don't feel well

_____ Excessive monitoring of health-related behaviors (excessively tracking your vitamin intake, the nutritional value of foods, the exercises you engage in)

What other approach safety behaviors do you use?

_____

## Avoidance Safety Behaviors

_____ Avoiding reading or watching anything related to illness, disease, or death

_____ Avoiding going for regular medical checkups

_____ Avoiding going for recommended assessments or tests (blood work, colonoscopy)

_____ Avoiding exercise, intense heat, or certain foods that might lead to various bodily symptoms

What other avoidance safety behaviors do you use?

_____

With this information in hand, you're ready to start identifying specific behavioral experiments.

## *IAD-Specific Behavioral Experiments*

Having occasional health complaints that might require medical intervention is a normal part of life: we expect to monitor our health for potentially serious problems when appropriate and to have regular checkups with a doctor as needed. The goal of behavioral experiments for IAD is therefore a bit more complex. Specifically, the goal is not to completely eliminate checking of physical symptoms, nor is it to seek out medical assistance whenever any change in health status occurs. Rather, it's to incorporate healthy standards of care into our lives while tolerating the uncertainty of unexplained minor physical symptoms.

If you're someone who tends to engage in approach safety behaviors, the goal of your behavioral experiments is twofold: first, to test out negative beliefs about uncertainty and become more comfortable with some uncertainty around bodily changes by not immediately engaging in safety behaviors whenever a physical sensation is experienced; second, to learn to make decisions about your health that are based on rational choices rather than driven by anxiety. Although we sometimes need to go to the doctor for tests, we want to ensure we go only when necessary, instead of seeking out a doctor's opinion every time we experience a minor physical change.

If instead you're someone who avoids the uncertainty of physical changes through avoidant safety behaviors, the goal of your behavioral experiments will be to test out feared predictions about uncertain medical testing, as well as to develop a more balanced approach to your overall health. Whereas people who engage in approach safety behaviors seek out excessive health information, those who use avoidant safety behaviors don't do it enough. Yet, since we'll all have some health problems in our lives, it's important to seek out medical consultations when needed. Moreover, we cannot avoid hearing about illness, disease, and death on occasion. As such, behavioral experiments targeting avoidance behaviors involve deliberately facing feared situations in order to test out feared outcomes (for example, that you have a serious illness).

# EXERCISE 8.8:
# Constructing Health Anxiety Behavioral Experiments

Because people with IAD cope with unexpected and unexplained bodily sensations by either seeking out health-related information or avoiding health-related triggers, there are two types of experiments that can be conducted.

### Experiments Targeting Approach Safety Behaviors

If you use approach safety behaviors—for example, looking up symptoms and medical information online or going for frequent doctor visits—these experiments will be most helpful for you.

A good first experiment is to follow the "three-day rule." When experiencing a mild unexplained bodily sensation (such as nausea or body aches), refrain from any kind of safety behavior for three days; that means no doctor visits, online searches, monitoring the area where you experienced the sensation, and asking for reassurance from others. After three days, if the physical sensation persists, you can decide whether you still want to go to the doctor or seek reassurance.

There are three exceptions to this rule: (1) if you experience a severe injury, such as a deep cut; (2) if you experience significant escalating pain or a sharp increase in the intensity of the physical sensation; or (3) if you experience common symptoms of a stroke (drooping face, arm weakness, slurred speech) or heart attack (severe chest pain or discomfort). In these cases, seek medical help immediately.

Additional IAD behavioral experiments are listed below. Go through each experiment and write down the level of anxiety (from 0 to 10) you would expect to feel if you faced that situation.

_____ Wait three days (or one week _____, or one month _____) before following up with a doctor about any mild uncertain bodily sensation or symptom

_____ Leave home without your cell phone

_____ Don't do any research after experiencing a new bodily sign or symptom

_____ Avoid seeking reassurance from family members concerning a new bodily sign or symptom

_____ Avoid self-exams (probing body for lumps, doing a breast exam) for varied amounts of time (several hours, days, weeks)

_____ Don't assess pulse rate or blood pressure for varied amounts of time (several hours, days, weeks)

## Experiments Targeting Avoidance Safety Behaviors

If you don't seek out certainty about physical sensations but instead try to avoid reminders of illness, then the following experiments are likely to be helpful. Give each an anxiety rating from 0 to 10:

_____ Make an appointment to see your doctor if you have been putting it off

_____ Make an appointment for follow-up assessments or procedures that have been recommended (going for blood work)

_____ Read about health and health-related matters

_____ Watch a movie or read a book that involves someone struggling with a severe illness

What are some other behavioral experiments related to health anxiety that you can think of?

_____

_____

_____

## Developing Appropriate Health Habits

No matter what type of safety behavior you use most to deal with health-related worries, it's a good idea to identify appropriate health behaviors in which to regularly engage. This can include the number of checkups you have each year, as well as specific recommendations made by your doctor if you already have a health condition (for example, cholesterol or high blood pressure tests). If you aren't sure how often you should go for medical exams, ask your family doctor.

Write down the health guidelines that you think are appropriate for you and then review them with your doctor.

Number of medical checkups each year: _____

Type and frequency of other medical tests each year: _____

_____

_____

The guidelines that you identified can be your road map for managing your health in the long term and can be used in conjunction with the behavioral experiments described above. For example, you might decide to have a checkup twice a year and to have additional recommended tests, such as blood work to assess your thyroid levels, every four months. However, if you suddenly begin experiencing mild symptoms, such as fatigue, you can engage in a behavioral experiment by waiting three days before consulting your doctor or speaking to friends and family about this symptom.

Now that you have some ideas of behavioral experiments that are relevant to you, you're ready to start planning and conducting them in exercise 8.9.

Hopefully, you now have some ideas for different ways you can challenge your worries related to anxiety and anxiety-related disorders. This next exercise will help you set up and carry out your behavioral experiments and test out your beliefs about uncertainty.

---

# EXERCISE 8.9:
## Conducting Behavioral Experiments

As we've suggested in prior chapters, it's a good idea to aim to complete two or three experiments per week, starting with experiments that you would expect to cause you mild to moderate anxiety (scores of 3 or 4 out of 10), then moving on to more challenging experiments over time.

Because the behavioral experiments are slightly different for each of the anxiety disorders, we've amended the basic worksheet for each disorder as needed and provided some examples for each. You can use the blank worksheet provided at the end of the examples, keeping in mind that you might be tracking slightly different things for different disorders. However, no matter what type of experiment you're conducting, don't forget to fill in the first two columns *before* conducting your experiment by writing down what you'll be doing (experiment) and what you're worried will happen (feared outcome). *After* completing your experiment, fill in the last two columns by writing down what happened (actual outcome) and how you coped with the situation in the moment if the outcome was negative (coping).

# GAD Experiments

Because people with GAD fear the uncertainty in daily life situations, your behavioral experiments will be similar to those described in previous chapters. Use your responses from exercise 8.2 to help you identify experiments most appropriate for you. The goal of these experiments is to have the opportunity to test out whether uncertain daily life situations consistently lead to negative outcomes that are catastrophic and unmanageable. A couple of examples of GAD behavioral experiments are provided below.

| Experiment (what you will be doing) | Feared Outcome (what you are worried will happen) | Actual Outcome (what actually happened) | Coping (if the outcome was negative, how you handled it) |
|---|---|---|---|
| Walk by myself on a quiet street in the middle of the day (do not use avoidance safety behavior) | I'll be mugged or attacked; I'll be overwhelmed with anxiety the whole time. | I was very nervous at first whenever I saw someone else on the street. Nothing bad happened. A few people said hello to me during my walk. | N/A |
| Ask a colleague to take over the task of ordering supplies for the office (do not use safety behavior of doing everything myself) | He'll order the wrong supplies or forget something important, and I'll have to fix the problem, which will be a waste of time. | My colleague did a pretty good job of ordering office supplies. He made one mistake, where he ordered the wrong size paper for the printer. | I mentioned the error he made with paper size, and he volunteered to take care of it. The problem was quickly resolved with a phone call. |

## SAD Experiments

If you're someone who struggles with SAD, you likely fear the uncertainty of social or performance-based situations. As such, using the experiment examples you identified in exercise 8.4, you can now conduct an experiment in which you deliberately face the uncertainty of a social situation without using your typical safety behaviors. Remember that it's important to describe your feared outcome in *concrete and observable terms*, so you can properly test out your fears. Some examples of SAD experiments are provided below.

| Experiment (what you will be doing) | Feared Outcome (what you are worried will happen) | Actual Outcome (what actually happened) | Coping (if the outcome was negative, how you handled it) |
|---|---|---|---|
| *Say no when colleagues ask me to go for lunch with them (do not use safety behavior of never saying no or excessively apologizing and explaining)* | *My colleagues will be mad at me. I'll know this because they won't talk to me after lunch and won't invite me out again.* | *Told them I wasn't able to go. One of my colleagues asked me why I couldn't make it. He looked concerned but didn't seem mad at me. A couple of my colleagues did chat with me after they came back from lunch. I did get invited out with them the next day.* | *When I was asked why I wasn't coming, I told my colleague I had a few things I had to get done. He said he understood.* |
| *Start a conversation with a barista at the coffee shop (do not use safety behavior of avoiding eye contact or small talk)* | *She will be annoyed and find me boring. I'll know this because she'll do things like roll her eyes, not smile, or cut the conversation short.* | *The conversation went really well! She smiled and looked interested, and after I paid for my coffee, she kept talking to me for a while.* | *N/A* |

# OCD Experiments

If you experience obsessions of doubt, harm to others, or contamination, you're likely concerned about the uncertainty around safety in situations where it's possible (even if highly improbable) that danger could occur. Using your responses from exercise 8.6, identify relevant experiments. A few OCD behavioral experiments are presented below. Try to repeat the same OCD experiment several times in order to draw conclusions about the actual danger of uncertain situations.

| Experiment (what you will be doing) | Feared Outcome (what you are worried will happen) | Actual Outcome (what actually happened) | Coping (if the outcome was negative, how you handled it) |
|---|---|---|---|
| Leave for work before my husband without phoning to remind him to check that all the doors and windows are closed and locked before he leaves (do not use safety behavior of excessive checking with others) | If I don't remind my husband or check in with him, he'll leave a window open or the patio door unlocked and someone will break in and rob us. | Husband left kitchen window open and unlocked. | Despite window being left open, no one broke in. Upset with husband, but no coping needed. House was fine. |
| Let son play at the playground (do not use avoidance safety behavior of not letting him go places where he might get hurt) | Son will fall off the play structure and break a bone or get a brain injury from hitting his head. | Son did fall and scrape both his knees when he was running around. | Brought son home, cleaned his wounds, and put on some bandages. He was upset but calmed down quickly. Scrapes don't seem too bad; was hard to see him upset, but he was having fun before he fell. |
| Go to mall and touch door handles (do not use avoidance safety behavior or wash excessively for at least 30 minutes after) | I will contract a serious illness or get very sick. | Feeling anxious not knowing if sick, but no signs so far. | Feeling anxious, but tried to sit with it. Still not completely sure if I did or didn't contract anything, but no signs of being sick so far. |

# IAD Experiments

People with IAD tend to fear the uncertainty of unexplained bodily sensations. The goal of IAD behavioral experiments is therefore to test whether the uncertainty associated with unexplained sensations is always negative and catastrophic, as well as to develop more appropriate standards for managing your health in the long term.

If you use approach safety behaviors to cope with health worries, start with the three-day rule (explained in detail earlier in this chapter). Here are some examples of this behavioral experiment in action.

| Unexplained Bodily Sensation and Experiment | Feared Outcome (what you are worried will happen) | Actual Outcome After Three Days (what actually happened) | Coping (what you did after the three days passed) |
|---|---|---|---|
| Experiencing pain in my stomach—sit with the sensation for three days | What if it's stomach cancer or some other serious disease? | The pain in my stomach went away after a day. | Decided not to go to the doctor since pain went away. |
| Experiencing discomfort in my arm after helping a friend move—sit with it for three days | What if I have seriously injured my arm? | After three days, I was still experiencing arm discomfort, but less than I originally did. | Decided to see the doctor, but felt less anxious overall. She told me that I had a very mild muscle strain and that the sensation would resolve within a few days. |

If you're more likely to engage in avoidance behaviors around health and unexplained bodily sensations, your behavioral experiments, like the examples provided here, will involve deliberately facing the uncertainty of the situation without engaging in safety behaviors.

| Experiment (what you will be doing) | Feared Outcome (what you are worried will happen) | Actual Outcome (what actually happened) | Coping (if the outcome was negative, how you handled it) |
|---|---|---|---|
| *Eat some cashews since my doctor told me I'm not allergic to them (not engaging in safety behavior of avoidance)* | *I'll have a deadly allergic reaction.* | *My throat felt scratchy after I ate the cashews.* | *I wanted to go to the hospital, but I drank some water and waited a little bit. The feeling of scratchiness went away.* |
| *Go to the doctor for a checkup (not engaging in avoidance)* | *I will find out I have a serious disease. I'll be so upset, I won't be able to handle it.* | *Doctor told me that I seemed fine, but sent me for blood tests as a part of the checkup.* | *I was very anxious about going for a blood test, but I went. The doctor told me everything came back normal.* |

Now that you have some examples of behavioral experiments, you can use the worksheet that follows to record your own experiments (also available as a PDF at http://www.newharbinger.com/40064). Please note that some of the columns of the worksheet will be completed a bit differently depending upon the particular disorder (changes to the column headings are noted with an asterisk).

| Experiment* (what you will be doing) *IAD: Unexplained Bodily Sensation and Experiment | Feared Outcome* (what you are worried will happen) *SAD: Feared Outcome and Observable Behavior | Actual Outcome* (what actually happened) *IAD: Actual Outcome After Three Days | Coping* (if the outcome was negative, how you handled it) *IAD: What You Did After the Three Days Passed |
|---|---|---|---|
| | | | |
| | | | |
| | | | |
| | | | |
| | | | |
| | | | |

As we've highlighted throughout this workbook, the only way to change your beliefs about uncertainty is to gather evidence that might challenge or contradict them. It's therefore important to consistently take stock of the evidence when conducting experiments. We recommend that you complete exercise 8.10 at the end of each week, since it will give you a chance to review the findings of your experiments.

---

# EXERCISE 8.10:
## Reviewing the Evidence

Because the overarching goal of behavioral experiments is to give you the opportunity to discover what actually happens when you deliberately face uncertainty, it's important to regularly review what you've uncovered so far. Specifically, you'll want to evaluate whether your belief that uncertainty leads to catastrophic and unmanageable negative outcomes is in fact accurate. To help with this, a number of questions are provided below, most of which can be answered regardless of what type of experiments you've been conducting, although there are a few disorder-specific questions. Complete this exercise at the end of each week (using the downloadable questionnaire at http://www.newharbinger.com/40064).

How many experiments did you conduct? _____

How often was the actual outcome positive or neutral? _____

_____

_____

How often was the actual outcome negative? _____

_____

_____

When (and if) the outcomes were negative, were they as bad as expected? _____

_____

_____

When (and if) the outcomes were negative, how do you think you handled the situation?

_____

_____

_____

If you completed SAD behavioral experiments, please answer these additional questions:

How did others respond to you when you took a social risk and faced an uncertain situation without using your usual safety behaviors?

_____

_____

_____

_____

What did you notice about yourself when you took a social risk and did not engage in your usual safety behaviors (for example, did you feel more genuine or spontaneous, or less constricted)?

_____

_____

_____

_____

If you completed IAD behavioral experiments, please answer these additional questions:

If you completed the three-day rule behavioral experiment, how often did you decide to seek reassurance, information, or medical advice at the end of three days?

_____

_____

_____

If you did seek out medical advice after sitting with the uncertainty of an unexplained bodily sensation for three days, was the outcome negative? If so, was it as bad as expected?

_____

_____

_____

_____

Regardless of whether or not you sought out reassurance, information, or medical advice after three days, did it feel different to make that decision after sitting with the anxiety for three days rather than attempting to reduce or eliminate uncertainty right away (for example, did you feel less anxious)?

_____

_____

_____

_____

Considering all the experiments you have done to date, answer the following:

What are the results of your experiments telling you about the outcomes of uncertain situations and your ability to handle them?

_____

_____

_____

_____

One of the main goals of this workbook is to help you develop balanced beliefs about the threat of uncertain situations in order to worry less. When you feel you have lots of behavioral experiments under your belt, it's a good time to gather all of your evidence to date, take stock of your findings, and begin the process of really evaluating the accuracy of your beliefs about uncertainty. The next section will help you do that.

## Taking Stock of Your Findings

By now you've hopefully had significant opportunities to test out your beliefs about uncertainty related to the anxiety disorder you're coping with. Looking back across all of the behavioral experiments you've conducted, what have you learned about the uncertainty related to your specific anxiety disorder? With all the information you've gathered so far, do you feel that you are starting to look at uncertainty differently now? And most importantly, do you find that you're worrying less and feeling less anxious? It's a good idea to consolidate all the evidence you've collected so far so you can use that information to begin to draw some overall conclusions. The next exercise will help you reflect on the information that you've gathered so far.

# EXERCISE 8.11:
## Taking Stock

Armed with the information obtained from all of the experiments you've completed to date, reflect back on your findings to answer the following questions (this questionnaire is also available at http://www.newharbinger.com/40064).

Do you find uncertainty as threatening as you did before? _____

_____

Are you more willing to face uncertain situations? _____

_____

Have you been engaging in fewer safety behaviors? _____

_____

Do you have more confidence in your ability to handle negative outcomes? _____

_____

Are you worrying less or feeling less anxious? _____

_____

_____

Have other people commented on changes they are seeing in you? _____

_____

_____

Noticing changes can be a big motivator for continuing to challenge and modify your beliefs related to uncertainty. If you haven't yet noticed any changes, you may just need more time, particularly if you're dealing with more than one disorder.

# When to Seek Professional Help

Although completing the experiments in this chapter can be very helpful in reducing disorder-specific worries, it's likely that these exercises will not be sufficient to completely overcome an anxiety disorder, especially if your symptoms are moderate to severe. Because of this, if you find yourself struggling or having difficulty utilizing the strategies introduced in this workbook, it can be very beneficial to seek professional help.

We recommend that you speak with your family doctor and find a therapist who specializes in cognitive behavioral therapy, as this type of psychological treatment has been shown to be effective in treating anxiety disorders (Hofmann et al. 2012). The good news is that even if you're at the point of seeking professional help, the information you learned so far can provide a solid foundation for the next steps in managing your worry and anxiety.

# In a Nutshell

This chapter focused on strategies for individuals who have been diagnosed with, or think they may have, an anxiety or anxiety-related disorder. By learning core strategies tailored to your specific disorder, you can acquire additional tools for successfully managing your worry. Here are the key points:

- Although different anxiety disorders have different "threats" that trigger anxiety and the content of the worry, they are all related to intolerance of uncertainty.

- Anxiety disorders are linked not only to a general intolerance of uncertainty, but also to disorder-specific intolerance of uncertainty. That is, individuals diagnosed with different disorders hold negative beliefs about specific uncertainties related to their disorder.

- Behavioral experiments are an important tool in managing the worry in anxiety disorders. Conducting appropriate behavioral experiments involves making specific predictions related to uncertainty, identifying disorder-specific safety behaviors, and then facing uncertain situations in order to test predictions of what will happen in those situations when not engaging in safety behaviors.

- Regardless of whether or not you've been diagnosed with an anxiety or anxiety-related disorder, managing excessive worry and anxiety on your own can be challenging. If you are having difficulty utilizing the strategies on your own, it can be beneficial to seek professional help.

Now that you've had a chance to tackle worry related to various anxiety or anxiety-related disorders, it's time to figure out how to maintain your gains and take steps toward bringing together all you've learned in order to live a richer and fuller life.

# CHAPTER 9

# Inviting Uncertainty into Your Life: Accepting Risk and Building Self-Confidence

The primary goal of this workbook has been to help you change your relationship with uncertainty in order to ultimately feel less worried and anxious. In this final chapter, we want to turn your attention to the road ahead by looking at how to continue managing your worries in the future, but also how to enrich your life by accepting uncertainty as a potential opportunity for personal growth. This chapter therefore discusses strategies for maintaining your gains and building on your progress. We'll also review acceptable risks in uncertain situations, the benefits of embracing uncertainty, and ways to build self-confidence.

## Facing Uncertainty in the Long Term

Hopefully by now you've completed lots of behavioral experiments and have begun to not only worry less, but change the way you behave in situations that were previously anxiety-provoking. Perhaps it's easier now to make small decisions or share your opinion. However, as important as it is for you to notice changes while you're actively working on managing your worries, it's even more important for those changes to endure.

### *Maintaining Gains over Time*

One of the best ways to maintain your gains and build on your current progress is to continue practicing the skills you've learned. Completing the exercises throughout this workbook is a great start, especially if you've already noticed some changes, but you're probably not all the way there. As such, it's a good idea to have a plan for the weeks and months ahead. In the next exercise, you'll take a step back and look at which worries and safety behaviors remain problematic so that you can make a plan of action to tackle them moving forward.

# EXERCISE 9.1:
# Taking Stock of Your Progress

The goal of this exercise is to identify where you were and where you are now in terms of worry themes and safety behaviors. First, take at least one week to record your worries and safety behaviors using the monitoring form in exercise 3.1.

After completing a week of tracking, it's time to look at which excessive worries remain. Using the list of worry topics below, ask yourself: (1) Was this topic a problem in the past? (2) Is this topic a problem now? (3) If it's a problem now, is it a normal worry given the circumstances? This last question is a reminder that not all worries are excessive but are sometimes appropriate given the situation, like worrying about your health when you're currently undergoing medical testing.

## Worry Topics/Themes

### 1. Health/physical symptoms:

Was this topic a problem in the past? _____

Is this topic a problem now? _____

If it's a problem now, is it a normal worry given the circumstances? _____

### 2. Danger/safety:

Was this topic a problem in the past? _____

Is this topic a problem now? _____

If it's a problem now, is it a normal worry given the circumstances? _____

### 3. Social situations:

Was this topic a problem in the past? _____

Is this topic a problem now? _____

If it's a problem now, is it a normal worry given the circumstances? _____

### 4. Work/school:

Was this topic a problem in the past? _____

Is this topic a problem now? _____

If it's a problem now, is it a normal worry given the circumstances? _____

### 5. Interpersonal relationships:

Was this topic a problem in the past? _____

Is this topic a problem now? _____

If it's a problem now, is it a normal worry given the circumstances? _____

### 6. Daily activities and responsibilities:

Was this topic a problem in the past? _____

Is this topic a problem now? _____

If it's a problem now, is it a normal worry given the circumstances? _____

## 7. Decision making:

Was this topic a problem in the past? _____

Is this topic a problem now? _____

If it's a problem now, is it a normal worry given the circumstances? _____

## 8. Perfectionism:

Was this topic a problem in the past? _____

Is this topic a problem now? _____

If it's a problem now, is it a normal worry given the circumstances? _____

Write out the worry topics or themes that remain problematic for you:

_____

_____

In addition to listing your remaining problematic worries (if any), identify the safety behaviors you still engage in. Remember that safety behaviors involve actions taken to reduce worry and anxiety. For example, avoiding going to a party because you'd rather stay home to get a good night's sleep is not a safety behavior; however, avoiding a party because you're worried you won't know what to say to people *is* a safety behavior. Read through the following list of common safety behaviors and check all the ones you still engage in.

### Safety Behaviors

_____ Avoidance

_____ Procrastination

_____ Impulsive decision making

_____ Partial commitment

_____ Delegating responsibility to others

_____ Doing everything yourself (not delegating tasks)

_____ Excessive reassurance seeking

_____ Checking

_____ Excessive information seeking

_____ Excessive preparation

Armed with the knowledge of what worries and safety behaviors remain problematic, you're ready to set up exercises for the weeks ahead.

---

## Obstacles to Progress

It can be challenging to consistently and regularly complete the exercises in this workbook in order to see long-term benefits. There are a number of obstacles that can impede your progress.

First, when working on managing worry and anxiety on your own, *you're only accountable to yourself.* Because of this, it's easy to tell yourself that you'll complete an exercise and then simply not do it. This is one of the benefits of seeing a therapist, since you know that your therapist will ask about what exercises you've completed. When we know that we're accountable to someone else, we're more likely to follow through. It's therefore important to increase personal accountability by *becoming your own therapist.*

Second, practicing skills over the long term involves the *ability to stick with a new routine.* Most of us are able to integrate something new into our schedule for a few weeks, but we often slip back into our old routine as time passes. We're more likely to stick with an activity, though, if we make it a *habit.* Habits are formed when we engage in a particular activity repeatedly and in the same context (Lally and Gardner 2013). For instance, every time you get into your car (context), you buckle your seat belt (activity). The benefit of habits is that they're almost automatic, which means we do them without thinking about it. The challenge, however, is in making a habit out of a relatively new behavior.

Given these obstacles, the best way to achieve long-term success is to become your own therapist and make your worry management exercises a habit. The next exercise will help you do this.

# EXERCISE 9.2:
# Developing an Ongoing Plan of Action

This exercise is meant to help you develop an action plan for managing worry over the long term. Given that things can change over time, you can expect to revise and adjust the content of your plan when needed.

## Step 1: Setting the Stage

To increase accountability (and become your own therapist), plan a regular weekly session with yourself. Give yourself at least thirty minutes of uninterrupted time. You can have your session anywhere, but make sure to minimize distractions (such as turning off your cell phone). You might decide to go to a coffee shop, treat yourself to a favorite drink, and create a sense of occasion around your session. Write down the time and place of your first session.

Date & time: _____

Location: _____

## Step 2: Setting the Agenda

As part of becoming your own therapist, you'll need to set a structure to your sessions. The agenda for each session should include a review of what you did since your last session, any observations from prior exercises, and plans for new exercises. Fill out the sections below to set the stage for your first session.

### Plan of Action Agenda: First Session

*What areas of life do I need to work on?*

Problematic worry topics or themes: _____

_____

_____

Problematic safety behaviors I still use: _____

_____

_____

*What experiments can I conduct to address these problem areas?*

For example, if you continue to worry a great deal about making decisions at work and often either procrastinate or ask someone else to make the decisions, a good experiment would be to make two or three small decisions a week without procrastinating.

List the experiments or workouts you plan to conduct over the upcoming week:

1. _____

2. _____

3. _____

Make sure to set a regular session time for yourself, preferably in the same place, in order to establish a routine. In addition, take notes on the outcome of your weekly sessions.

Now that you have some ideas for exercises for the coming week, you can set the date for your next session.

**Next plan of action session:**

Date & time: _____

Location: _____

## *Plan of Action Agenda: Weekly Session*

Below is a template (available at http://www.newharbinger/40064) of what your weekly sessions might include, although you can adjust the content of your sessions over time according to your progress and what you need to work on.

Date: _____

*What experiments did I complete since the last session?*

1. _____

2. _____

3. _____

*Looking at all the experiments I have conducted to date, what observations can I make about my beliefs about uncertainty?*

How many experiments have I conducted so far? _____

How often was the outcome negative? _____

_____

How often was the outcome neutral or positive? _____

_____

When the outcome was negative, how often was it catastrophic or severe? _____

_____

_____

When the outcome was negative, how often was I able to cope with the situation? _____

_____

Looking at all the times I had to cope with a negative situation, how did I handle the situations overall? Did I cope well? Was I able to figure out how to deal with negative consequences?

_____

_____

_____

*What exercises will I be conducting over the coming week?*

1. _____

2. _____

3. _____

**Next plan of action session:**

Date & time: _____

Location: _____

If you find that you've stopped engaging in tolerating uncertainty exercises or you're falling back into old patterns, that's okay. Lapses happen. One of the great things about CBT skills is that you can pick them back up at any time. So if you feel like you've lost ground on your progress, flip back to any chapter of this book and get right back on track. You always have the tools for managing worry in your back pocket, and you can pull them out whenever you need them.

# Embracing Uncertainty: Risk and Rewards

Throughout this workbook, we've discussed the importance of overcoming the fear of uncertainty in order to worry less. Research shows that when you reduce your intolerance to uncertainty, a reduction in worry follows (Bomyea et al. 2015; Dugas et al. 1998). Yet beyond the benefit of worrying less, becoming more tolerant of uncertainty can have far-reaching effects (both negative and positive) on our lives. Therefore, it's important to have an idea about what you're getting into when you invite uncertainty into your life.

## Living a Life with Uncertainty

There's no denying that trying to achieve certainty in order to cope with worries has an impact on your life. Picture your life as a huge open field where you can walk anywhere. When you try to avoid uncertainties in life, you're putting up a fence around yourself. The space within the fence might seem wide at first, but your life is essentially contained within the boundaries of the fence: you don't walk beyond the fence, and over time, you might stop thinking about what lies there. Moreover, the fence doesn't stay in the same place: it tends to close in over time as you become more fearful of uncertainty, which can make your world (and the places where you feel safe) very limited. When you started engaging in behavioral experiments and deliberately invite uncertainty into your life, you started pushing back that fence. But what lies beyond it?

When facing uncertainty, there's no escaping the fact that things can go awry. You probably discovered this when conducting behavioral experiments. Although uncertain events often turn out fine, there are occasions when a negative outcome does occur. We sometimes delegate tasks to our children and they don't do them, or we order a new meal in a restaurant and don't like it. In other words, inviting uncertainty into your life involves some risk. However, it also has the potential for great reward.

When you allow uncertainty into your life, there's the possibility that you might meet a romantic partner, discover a new interest, or just enjoy the spontaneous pleasures that a full life can offer. This invites the questions: is it worth it? Do the benefits of leading a fuller life outweigh the risks of negative outcomes on occasion? The next exercise will give you the opportunity to think through these questions.

# EXERCISE 9.3:
# Is a Life Without Certainty Worth the Risk?

In this exercise, you'll contrast the risks and benefits of inviting uncertainty into your life by reviewing the behavioral experiments you've completed to date. This will allow you to evaluate the risks and rewards associated with facing uncertainty. Answer the following questions using all of your behavioral experiment worksheets to date. (A PDF of this form is available at http://www.newharbinger .com/40064.)

1. How many experiments have you conducted so far? _____

2. How many experiments had a negative outcome? _____

3. Calculate the percentage of negative outcomes overall* _____

    *  *Multiply the number of experiments with a negative outcome by 100 and divide by the total number of experiments; for example, if you completed 40 experiments and 5 had a negative outcome, the percentage of negative outcomes overall would be 12.5%.*

4. Calculate the percentage of neutral or positive outcomes* _____

    *  *Subtract the percentage you calculated for negative outcomes from 100; for example, 100 − 12.5% = 87.5%.*

5. What were some of the worst outcomes that occurred during your experiments?

    _____

    _____

    _____

Now let's compare the negative outcomes you've experienced to the positive or neutral outcomes.

6. What were some of the best outcomes that occurred during your experiments?

    _____

    _____

    _____

7.   What changes have you seen in your life since inviting in more uncertainty? (To answer this question, think about your current level of worry and anxiety, new experiences or opportunities, or time saved.)

_____

_____

_____

_____

8.   Looking at the percentage of times you've had a negative outcome versus the percentage of times you've had a positive outcome, the worst negative outcome you've experienced versus the best uncertain outcome you've had, as well as the benefits you've received from inviting uncertainty into your life, do you find that the rewards outweigh the costs or vice versa?

_____

_____

_____

_____

As you continue to conduct behavioral experiments and tolerating uncertainty workouts, you can view this exercise as an ongoing evaluation of the impact, both positive and negative, that uncertainty has on your life. You might decide to include this exercise in your action plan from exercise 9.2, perhaps once a month.

## Identifying Reasonable Risks

There are risks in almost everything we do. When we're standing on the sidewalk of a quiet residential street, most of us don't find this particularly dangerous. Yet we can't be 100 percent certain that a car won't suddenly swerve up onto the sidewalk and hit us. Why isn't this uncertain situation threatening? It has to do with the difference between a *possible* versus a *probable* threat. That is, although it's possible that a car could suddenly swerve up and hit us, it's highly unlikely.

But the fact remains that many things are possible. For this reason, seeking certainty in life is an exercise in futility: there's very little we can be entirely certain of, such that most threats are possible, even if very unlikely. When any uncertain situation that has the *possibility* of a negative outcome is viewed as threatening, it makes the world seem like a very dangerous place. This is not to say that we should never be fearful of uncertain situations. If you spot a cougar while on a hike, you aren't certain it will attack you. Yet the probability that it might attack you is high enough that most people would find it an anxiety-provoking situation.

So what is a reasonable risk? Typically, situations where the probability of a catastrophic negative outcome is extremely low, or where a more probable negative outcome is relatively minor, are considered reasonable risks. For example, if you decide to take a tango class, there's the very improbable risk that you'll make such a complete fool of yourself that others will laugh hysterically at you. There's the more probable risk that you'll not master the steps right away and feel awkward. However, there's also the potential that it will be fun. In general, it's important to remember that most uncertain situations carry some risk, but just because a negative outcome is possible doesn't mean it's probable.

## Moving Toward Embracing Uncertainty

Throughout this workbook, we've discussed the importance of learning to tolerate uncertainty in order to reduce your worries. However, the word "tolerance" suggests you can learn to live with something even though it's unpleasant. For example, you might tolerate the presence of mosquitoes when camping, but you do so in order to enjoy the outdoors. In other words, tolerance suggests that there's something inherently negative about the situation. But is this really the case?

Think about the pleasure of unexpectedly finding a ten-dollar bill in a pair of jeans, the surprise of opening a present, or the happiness you feel when you meet someone special. These are all examples of uncertain situations, yet they're all pleasant. It's easy to forget that uncertain situations carry the potential for positive outcomes and opportunities. It's important to think beyond simply "tolerating" and consider the notion of embracing uncertainty.

You might have already discovered through your own behavioral experiments that when you allow uncertainty into your life, you open yourself up to experiences you might not have normally had. Perhaps you tried a new kind of food you ended up loving, or you enhanced your relationship with your children and increased their self-confidence by trusting them to take on new responsibilities. Although the strategies in this workbook are designed to help you decrease your worry and anxiety, when you give yourself the chance to embrace the uncertainties of life, you can live a richer life.

# Learning to Trust Yourself

You already know that attempting to seek certainty in life comes at a cost. Worrying excessively, being anxious, and engaging in safety behaviors can be exhausting and can reduce your quality of life. But there is another cost to the search for certainty that's less obvious. Specifically, efforts to reduce or avoid uncertainty in your life also have a significant impact on your self-confidence.

## *Uncertainty and Self-Confidence*

Safety behaviors are used to reduce or eliminate uncertainty, but by using them, we're deliberately not trusting our own judgment. Let's say Dana has to decide what to make for a dinner party. She could decide to make something she thinks her guests will like. Alternatively, Dana could call all of her guests to find out exactly what they like. If Dana decides what to make, she is placing trust in her own judgment and displaying confidence in her ability to host an enjoyable dinner party. In the latter scenario, Dana doesn't have to trust herself: she effectively eliminates any chance that her friends might not like the dinner by asking everyone what they prefer. By favoring certainty, Dana doesn't have to worry that her guests won't like what she prepared since she already knows their preferences. However, she has inadvertently told herself that she can't trust her own judgment. Trusting ourselves is based not on certainty, but on the belief that we can make rational, thoughtful choices.

Worry also impacts our trust in ourselves. When we worry, we're thinking about all the potential negative outcomes of an uncertain situation and the different ways we might cope with those outcomes. If you're worried about bad weather during a planned beach day, you might think about all the alternate options for activities. This attempt to mentally plan for negative outcomes before they've even occurred is akin to telling yourself that you're incapable of handling any unforeseen event unless you've already thought about and planned for it ahead of time. It's this aspect of worry, as well as the safety behaviors that it engenders, that prevents us from finding out about our ability to cope with negative outcomes in the moment. It is only when you invite uncertainty into your life that you're able to see that you can trust yourself to handle unexpected outcomes as they arise.

# Building Self-Confidence

In the 1970s, psychologist Albert Bandura identified the concept of *self-efficacy*, which refers to our belief in our ability to accomplish something successfully. If you have self-efficacy regarding your sense of direction, for example, you can confidently drive to new locations believing that even if you get lost, you can orient yourself and find your way. Self-efficacy is a part of self-confidence, and it has a significant impact on our actions.

In general, we're less likely to engage in a task if we have low self-efficacy, irrespective of our actual ability (Bandura 1986, 1997). If you have low self-efficacy about decision making, you're likely to avoid making decisions, regardless of your actual abilities. This means that our perception of our abilities not only influences our behavior, but impacts our sense of self-confidence. If we don't think we're able to do something, we're less likely to try and more likely to think that we'd be unsuccessful if we did.

So how do we build self-confidence? Bandura (1977) noted that one of the most influential sources of self-efficacy comes from actual experience. That is, we're more confident in our ability to do something when we have the experience of having done it in the past. If you've been driving for a while, you probably have good self-efficacy about your driving ability because you have lots of experience driving and, over time, you developed a sense of mastery.

Yet safety behaviors prevent you from finding out how an uncertain situation would have turned out—and how you would have handled any negative outcomes—if you had allowed yourself to face uncertainty. It's for this reason that behavioral experiments can have such a strong impact on your self-confidence: by deliberately entering into uncertain situations, you give yourself the opportunity to learn about your ability firsthand. That is, through your own direct experience, you can learn to trust yourself by seeing how you handle unexpected events.

Remember that time and experience can lead to a sense of mastery in various aspects of your life. It's only when we truly trust ourselves and our own judgment that we cease to worry excessively, and this is simply because we no longer feel the need to worry.

# In a Nutshell

In this chapter, we focused on what you want in your future life beyond simply worrying less. Here are some key points:

- In order to maintain your gains and continue to make progress, you need to consistently practice the skills you've learned.

- It can be challenging to practice skills over the long term, so it's important to become your own "therapist" by scheduling your own weekly sessions.

- Try to move from tolerating to embracing uncertainty in your life. Although there are always risks when facing uncertain situations, accepting reasonable risks enables us to enjoy the benefits of embracing uncertainty through new opportunities, new challenges, and the chance to live a richer and fuller life.

- Acceptable risks involve situations where the chance of a negative outcome is very unlikely or a more probable negative outcome is minor.

- When you embrace uncertainty, you get the added benefit of increasing your self-confidence. Worrying and engaging in safety behaviors interfere with the opportunity to develop trust in your own decisions and abilities.

- Self-efficacy, a component of self-confidence, is your perception of your abilities in specific situations. When you have good self-efficacy, you're more likely to engage in tasks with confidence because you have more trust in your abilities.

- One of the best ways to build self-efficacy is through experience. By continuing to engage in behavioral experiments and deliberately dropping your safety behaviors, you have the opportunity to increase your self-efficacy by actually observing how you manage negative outcomes when they arise.

As a final point, remember that learning how to manage your worry and anxiety means facing things that are uncertain and proving to yourself that you can cope. Life is filled with uncertainty, which is not a bad thing. Embracing the uncertainties in life enables us to make discoveries, be surprised, and enjoy a fuller life. We hope that you take these skills with you and not only worry less, but enjoy life more.

# Acknowledgments

There are several people who have been invaluable in shaping the development and content of this book. First, I would like to greatly thank my coauthor, Kristin Buhr, for getting involved in this project with me. We have worked together for over fifteen years now, first in Montreal, then in Vancouver, and I hope we continue to do so for many years to come. Kristin, I greatly appreciate your knowledge and clinical expertise, as well as your enduring friendship.

As with all the work I have done in psychology, I am extremely grateful to Dr. Michel Dugas for his guidance and support. Most of the ideas developed in this workbook are either directly or indirectly related to the excellent research that he and his research team have conducted over the years. Michel, I can't thank you enough for continuing to work with me and for being so supportive of my endeavours. You are a brilliant researcher and academic, and a wonderful friend.

I have been fortunate to work with many excellent researchers and clinicians across my career, and their knowledge and insight were an invaluable resource while writing this book. In Montreal, I would like to thank everyone in the Anxiety Disorders Laboratory, including Naomi Koerner, Nina Laugesen, Mary Hedayati, Kathryn Sexton, and Kylie Francis. Special thanks to Dr. Adam Radomsky, who helped me so many times and continues to be a great (and hilarious) friend. In Vancouver, I would like to thank Drs. Maureen Whittal, Jack Rachman, and Peter McLean for their mentorship and guidance when I first started out in the field of CBT and anxiety, and all of my wonderful friends and colleagues at the Vancouver CBT Centre, including Drs. Brandy McGee, Rachael Lunt, Mark Lau, Fjola Helgadottir, Katherine Martinez, and Rachel Vella-Zarb. I would be remiss if I also didn't take the time to thank Marina Kononenko, who always makes our clinic a great place to work! My sincere gratitude to my good friends Dr. Sarah Newth, Dr. Clare Philips, and Arto Tienaho, all of whom have had to hear me talk about this book project since its inception.

Thanks to New Harbinger, and in particular Camille Hayes, for assisting Kristin and me throughout the process of completing this book and thereby allowing us to share our clinical ideas with others.

Finally, I would like to thank my family for their love, understanding, and support. In particular, I want to thank my mother, Carolyn, and my partner, Antony, for being there for me throughout my career. Over the years, you have both moved across the country with me, tolerated my crazy hours, and helped me get through difficult times, all in support of me and my work. My sincere love and gratitude to you both.

—Melisa Robichaud

I would like to thank Dr. Michel Dugas for his direction, support, and encouragement. I am extremely grateful for all of the opportunities you have given me. I also want to extend my appreciation to the members of the Anxiety Disorders Laboratory at Concordia University for their support and inspiration on many different levels. Much of the research we conducted in the lab has informed my clinical work and is the basis for many of the ideas in this workbook. I would especially like to thank Naomi Koerner, Kylie Francis, Nina Laugesen, Mary Hedayati, and Kathryn Sexton. My sincerest gratitude to my coauthor, Melisa Robichaud, for giving me the opportunity to write this book with her. I am tremendously grateful for your knowledge, support, and enduring friendship.

I would also like to thank some of the amazing mentors I have been fortunate to work with over the years, including Dr. Ron Norton, Dr. Peter McLean, Dr. Maureen Whittal, Dr. Jack Rachman, Dr. Lynn Alden, and Dr. Bill Koch.

I want to extend my gratitude to my amazing friends and colleagues, especially at the North Shore Stress and Anxiety Clinic, for sharing their expertise and offering their endless support. I feel extremely fortunate to be part of an amazing group of clinicians. A special thanks to my dear friend and colleague Dr. Sarah Newth. Your friendship and insight have been invaluable.

I would also like to thank the clients I have worked with over the years. I have learned a great deal from all of you, and it has been a privilege to be part of your journey.

Finally, I want to thank my parents, Ken and Lou-Anne, for their ongoing support and encouragement; my brother, Kevin, for paving the way; and my writing companions, Zoë and Dakota. I want to express my deepest gratitude to my husband, Dan, and my son, Logan, who enrich my life immensely. Thank you for your love, patience, and understanding.

—Kristin Buhr

# References

American Psychiatric Association (APA). 2013. *Diagnostic and Statistical Manual of Mental Disorders.* 5th ed. Washington, DC: American Psychiatric Association.

Antony, M., C. Purdon, V. Huta, and R. Swinson. 1998. "Dimensions of Perfectionism Across the Anxiety Disorders." *Behaviour Research and Therapy* 36: 1143–1154.

Antony, M., and R. Swinson. 2009. *When Perfect Isn't Good Enough: Strategies for Coping with Perfectionism.* 2nd ed. Oakland, CA: New Harbinger Publications.

Aronson, E., and J. Mills. 1959. "The Effect of Severity of Initiation on Liking for a Group." *Journal of Abnormal and Social Psychology* 59: 177–181.

Bandura, A. 1977. *Social Learning Theory.* Englewood/ Cliffs, NJ: Prentice Hall.

Bandura, A. 1986. *Social Foundations of Thought and Action: A Social Cognitive Theory.* Englewood Cliffs, NJ: Prentice Hall.

Bandura, A. 1997. *Self-Efficacy: The Exercise of Control.* New York: Freeman.

Barkley-Levenson, E. E., and C. R. Fox. 2016. "The Surprising Relationship Between Indecisiveness and Impulsivity." *Personality and Individual Differences* 90: 1–6. doi:10.1016/j.paid.2015.10.030.

Barsky, A. J., and J. F. Borus. 1995. "Somatization and Medicalization in the Era of Managed Care." *Journal of the American Medical Association* 274: 1931–1934.

Birrell, J., K. Meares, A. Wilkinson, and M. Freeston. 2011. "Toward a Definition of Intolerance of Uncertainty: A Review of Factor Analytical Studies of the Intolerance of Uncertainty Scale." *Clinical Psychology Review* 31: 1198–1208. doi:10.1016/j.cpr.2011.07.009.

Blakey, S. M., and J. S. Abramowitz. 2016. "The Effects of Safety Behaviors During Exposure Therapy for Anxiety: Critical Analysis from an Inhibitory Learning Perspective." *Clinical Psychology Review* 49: 1–15. https://doi.org/10.1016/j.cpr.2016.07.002.

Boelen, P. A., and R. N. Carleton. 2012. "Intolerance of Uncertainty, Hypochondriacal Concerns, OCD, and Worry." *Journal of Nervous and Mental Disease* 200: 208–213. http://dx.doi.org/10.1097/NMD.0b013e318247cb17.

Boelen, P. A., and A. Reijntjes. 2009. "Intolerance of Uncertainty and Social Anxiety." *Journal of Anxiety Disorders* 23: 130–135. https://doi.org/10.1016/j.janxdis.2008.04.007.

Bomyea, J., H. Ramsawh, T. M. Ball, C. T. Taylor, M. P. Paulus, and A. J. Lang. 2015. "Intolerance of Uncertainty as a Mediator of Reductions in Worry in a Cognitive Behavioral Treatment Program for Generalized Anxiety Disorder." *Journal of Anxiety Disorders* 33: 90–94. doi:10.1016/j.janxdis.2015.05.004.

Buhr, K., and M. J. Dugas. 2002. "The Intolerance of Uncertainty Scale: Psychometric Properties of the English Version." *Behaviour Research and Therapy* 40: 931–945. doi:10.1016/S0005-7967(01)00092-4.

Burns, D. 1980. "The Perfectionist's Script for Self-Defeat." *Psychology Today*, November, 34–51.

Carleton, R. N. 2016. "Fear of the Unknown: One Fear to Rule Them All?" *Journal of Anxiety Disorders* 41: 5–21. http:// dx.doi.org/10.1016/j.janxdis.2016.03.011.

Carleton, R. N., K. C. Collimore, and J. G. Asmundson. 2010. " 'It's Not Just the Judgements—It's That I Don't Know': Intolerance of Uncertainty as a Predictor of Social Anxiety." *Journal of Anxiety Disorders* 24: 189–195. https://doi.org/10.1016/j.janxdis.2009.10.007.

Carleton, R. N., S. Duranceau, M. H. Freeston, P. A. Boelen, R. E. McCabe, and M. M. Antony. 2014. " 'But It Might Be a Heart Attack': Intolerance of Uncertainty and Panic Disorder Symptoms." *Journal of Anxiety Disorders* 28: 463–470. https://doi.org/10.1016/j.janxdis.2014.04.006.

Carleton, R. N., M. K. Mulvogue, M. A. Thibodeau, R. E. McCabe, M. M. Antony, and G. J. G. Asmundson. 2012. "Increasingly Certain About Uncertainty: Intolerance of Uncertainty Across Anxiety and Depression." *Journal of Anxiety Disorders* 26: 468–479. https://doi.org/10.1016/j.janxdis.2012.01.011.

Clark, D. M., G. Butler, M. Fennell, A. Hackmann, F. McManus, and A. Wells. 1995. "Social Behavior Questionnaire." Unpublished manuscript.

Conroy, D. E., M. P. Kaye, and A. M. Fifer. 2007. "Cognitive Links Between Fear of Failure and Perfectionism." *Journal of Rational-Emotive and Cognitive-Behavior Therapy* 25: 237–253. doi:10.1007/s10942-007-0052-7.

Counsell, A., M. Furtado, C. Iorio, L. Anand, A. Canzonieri, A. Fine, K. Fotinos, I. Epstein, and M. A. Katzman. 2017. "Intolerance of Uncertainty, Social Anxiety, and Generalized Anxiety: Differences by Diagnosis and Symptoms." *Psychiatry Research* 252: 63–69. https://doi.org/10.1016/j.psychres.2017.02.046.

Dar-Nimrod, I., C. D. Rawn, D. R. Lehman, and B. Schwartz. 2009. "The Maximization Paradox: The Cost of Seeking Alternatives." *Personality and Individual Differences* 46: 631–635. doi:10.1016/j.paid.2009.01.007.

Dugas, M. J., F. Gagnon, R. Ladouceur, and M. H. Freeston. 1998. "Generalized Anxiety Disorder: A Preliminary Test of a Conceptual Model." *Behaviour Research and Therapy* 36: 215–226. doi:10.1016/S0005–7967(97)00070–3.

Dugas, M. J., H. Letarte, J. Rhéaume, M. H. Freeston, and R. Ladouceur. 1995. "Worry and Problem Solving: Evidence of a Specific Relationship." *Cognitive Therapy and Research* 19: 109–120. http://dx.doi.org/10.1007/BF02229679.

Dugas, M. J., A. Marchand, and R. Ladouceur. 2005. "Further Validation of a Cognitive-Behavioral Model of Generalized Anxiety Disorder: Diagnostic and Symptom Specificity." *Journal of Anxiety Disorders* 19: 329–343. doi:10.1016/j.janxdis.2004.02.002.

Dugas, M. J., and M. Robichaud. 2006. *Cognitive-Behavioral Treatment for Generalized Anxiety Disorder: From Science to Practice.* New York: Routledge.

Egan, S. J., T. D. Wade, and R. Shafron. 2011. "Perfectionism as a Transdiagnostic Process: A Clinical Review." *Clinical Psychology Review* 31: 203–212. https://doi.org/10.1016/j.cpr.2010.04.009.

Fergus, T. A., and D. P. Valentiner. 2011. "Intolerance of Uncertainty Moderates the Relationship Between Catastrophic Health Appraisals and Health Anxiety." *Cognitive Therapy and Research* 35: 560–565. doi:10.1007/s10608–011–9392–9.

Freeston, M. H., J. Rhéaume, H. Letarte, M. J. Dugas, and R. Ladouceur. 1994. "Why Do People Worry?" *Personality and Individual Differences* 17: 791–802. https://doi.org/10.1016/0191–8869(94)90048–5.

Frost, R. O., P. Marten, C. Lahart, and R. Rosenblate. 1990. "The Dimensions of Perfectionism." *Cognitive Therapy and Research* 14: 449–468. doi:10.1007/BF01172967.

Gentes, E. L., and A. M. Ruscio. 2011. "A Meta-analysis of the Relation of Intolerance of Uncertainty to Symptoms of Generalized Anxiety Disorder, Major Depressive Disorder, and Obsessive-Compulsive Disorder." *Clinical Psychology Review* 31: 923–933. https://doi.org/10.1016/j.cpr.2011.05.001.

Hamacheck, D. E. 1978. "Psychodynamics of Normal and Neurotic Perfectionism." *Psychology* 15: 27–33.

Handley, A. K., S. J. Egan, R. T. Kane, and C. S. Rees. 2014. "The Relationships Between Perfectionism, Pathological Worry and Generalized Anxiety Disorder." *BMC Psychiatry* 14: 98. doi:10.1186/1471–244X-14–98.

Helbig-Lang, S., and F. Petermann. 2010. "Tolerate or Eliminate? A Systematic Review on the Effects of Safety Behavior Across Anxiety Disorders." *Clinical Psychology Science and Practice* 17: 218–233. doi:10.1111/j.1468–2850.2010.01213.x.

Hirsch, C. R., T. Meynen, and D. M. Clark. 2004. "Negative Self-Imagery in Social Anxiety Contaminates Social Interactions." *Memory, Special Issues: Mental Imagery and Memory in Psychopathology* 12: 496–506.

Hofmann, S. G., A. Asnaani, I. J. J. Vonk, A. T. Sawyer, and A. Fang. 2012. "The Efficacy of Cognitive Behavioral Therapy: A Review of Meta-Analyses." *Cognitive Therapy and Research* 36: 427–440. doi:10.1007/s10608–012–9476–1.

Inglis, I. R. 2000. "The Central Role of Uncertainty Reduction in Determining Behaviour." *Behaviour* 137: 1567–1599.

Kawamura, K. Y., S. L. Hunt, R. O. Frost, and P. M. DiBartolo. 2001. "Perfectionism, Anxiety, and Depression: Are the Relationships Independent?" *Cognitive Therapy and Research* 25: 291–301. doi:10.1023/A:1010736529013.

Koerner, N., and M. J. Dugas. 2008. "An Investigation of Appraisals in Individuals Vulnerable to Excessive Worry: The Role of Intolerance of Uncertainty." *Cognitive Therapy and Research* 32: 619–638. doi:10.1007/s10608–007–9125–2.

Ladouceur, R., M. J. Dugas, M. H. Freeston, E. Léger, F. Gagnon, and N. Thibodeau. 2000. "Efficacy of a Cognitive-Behavioral Treatment for Generalized Anxiety Disorder: Evaluation in a Controlled Clinical Trial." *Journal of Consulting and Clinical Psychology* 68: 957–964. doi:10.1037/0022 –006X.68.6.957.

Ladouceur, R., M. J. Dugas, M. H. Freeston, J. Rhéaume, F. Blais, J.-M. Boisvert, F. Gagnon, and N. Thibodeau. 1999. "Specificity of Generalized Anxiety Disorder Symptoms and Processes." *Behavior Therapy* 30: 191–207. https://doi.org/10.1016/S0005–7894(99)80003–3.

Lally, P., and B. Gardner. 2013. "Promoting Habit Formation." *Health Psychology Review* 7: S137–S138. doi:10.1080/17437199.2011.603640.

Lee, A. Y. 2001. "The Mere Exposure Effect: An Uncertainty Reduction Explanation Revisited." *Personality and Social Psychology Bulletin* 10: 1255–1266.

Linkovski, O., E. Kalanthroff, A. Henik, and G. E. Anholt. 2016. "Stop Checking: Repeated Checking and Its Effects on Response Inhibition and Doubt." *Journal of Behaviour Therapy and Experimental Psychiatry* 53: 84–91. https://doi.org/10.1016/j.jbtep.2014.12.007.

McMillan, D., and R. Lee. 2010. "A Systematic Review of Behavioral Experiments vs. Exposure Alone in the Treatment of Anxiety Disorders: A Case of Exposure While Wearing the Emperor's New Clothes?" *Clinical Psychology Review* 30: 467–478.

Meeten, F., S. R. Dash, A. L. Scarlet, and G. C. Davey. 2012. "Investigating the Effect of Intolerance of Uncertainty on Catastrophic Worrying and Mood." *Behaviour Research and Therapy* 50: 690–698. http://dx.doi.org/10.1016/j.brat.2012.08. 003.

Misuraca, R., and U. Teuscher. 2013. "Time Flies When You Maximize: Maximizers and Satisficers Perceive Time Differently When Making Decisions." *Acta Psychologica* 143: 176–180. doi:10.1016/j.actpsy.2013.03.004.

Obsessive Compulsive Cognitions Working Group. 1997. "Cognitive Assessment of Obsessive-Compulsive Disorder." *Behaviour Research and Therapy* 35: 667–681. https://doi.org/10.1016/S0005-7967(97)00017-X.

Oglesby, M. E., J. W. Boffa, N. A. Short, A. M. Raines, and N. B. Schmidt. 2016. "Intolerance of Uncertainty as a Predictor of Post-traumatic Stress Symptoms Following a Traumatic Event." *Journal of Anxiety Disorders* 41: 82–87. http://dx.doi.org/10.1016/j.janxdis.2016.01.005.

Plasencia, M. L., L. E. Alden, and C. T. Taylor. 2011. "Differential Effects of Safety Behaviour Subtypes in Social Anxiety Disorder." *Behaviour Research and Therapy* 49: 665–675.

Radomsky, A. S., and G. M. Alcolado. 2010. "Don't Even Think About Checking: Mental Checking Causes Memory Distrust." *Experimental Psychiatry* 41: 345–351. https://doi.org/10.1016/j.jbtep.2010.03.005.

Radomsky, A. S., P. T. Gilchrist, and D. Dussault. 2006. "Repeated Checking Really Does Cause Memory Distrust." *Behaviour Research and Therapy* 44: 305–316. https://doi.org/10.1016/j.brat.2005.02.005.

Rassin, E., and P. Muris. 2005. "Indecisiveness and the Interpretation of Ambiguous Situations." *Personality and Individual Differences* 39: 1285–1291. doi:10.1016/j.paid.2005.06.006.

Rassin, E., P. Muris, I. Franken, M. Smit, and M. Wong. 2007. "Measuring General Indecisiveness." *Journal of Psychopathology and Behavioral Assessment* 29: 61–68.

Robichaud, M., and M. J. Dugas. 2015. *The Generalized Anxiety Disorder Workbook: A Comprehensive CBT Guide for Coping with Uncertainty, Worry, and Fear.* Oakland, CA: New Harbinger Publications.

Salkovskis, P. M. 1991. "The Importance of Behaviour in the Maintenance of Anxiety and Panic: A Cognitive Account." *Behavioural Psychotherapy* 19: 6–19.

Salkovskis, P. M., and H. M. C. Warwick. 1986. "Morbid Preoccupation, Health Anxiety and Reassurance: A Cognitive Behavioural Approach to Hypochondriasis." *Behaviour Research and Therapy* 24: 597–602.

Santanello, A. W., and F. L. Gardner. 2007. "The Role of Experiential Avoidance in the Relationship Between Maladaptive Perfectionism and Worry." *Cognitive Therapy and Research* 31: 319–332. doi:10.1007/s10608–006–9000–6.

Schwartz, B. 2004. "The Tyranny of Choice." *Scientific American*, April, 71–75.

Schwartz, B., A. Ward, J. Monterosso, S. Lyubomirsky, K. White, and D. R. Lehman. 2002. "Maximizing Versus Satisficing: Happiness Is a Matter of Choice." *Journal of Personality and Social Psychology* 83: 1178–1197. doi:10.1037//0022–3514.83.5.1178.

Sexton, K. A., and M. J. Dugas. 2009. "Defining Distinct Negative Beliefs About Uncertainty: Validating the Factor Structure of the Intolerance of Uncertainty Scale." *Psychological Assessment* 21: 176–186. doi:10.1037/a0015827.

Shafran, R., S. Egan, and T. Wade. 2010. *Overcoming Perfectionism: A Self-Help Guide Using Cognitive Behavioural Techniques.* London: Robinson Publishing.

Shihata, S., P. M. McEvoy, and B. A. Mullan. 2016. "Pathways from Uncertainty to Anxiety: An Evaluation of Hierarchical Model of Trait and Disorder-Specific Intolerance of Uncertainty on Anxiety Disorder Symptoms." *Journal of Anxiety Disorder* 45: 72–79. https://doi.org/10.1016/j.janxdis.2016.12.001.

Simon, H. A. 1955. "A Behavioral Model of Rational Choice." *Quarterly Journal of Economics* 59: 99–118.

Simon, H. A. 1956. "Rational Choice and the Structure of the Environment." *Psychological Review* 63: 129–138.

Simon, H. A. 1957. *Models of Man, Social and Rational: Mathematical Essays on Rational Human Behavior.* New York: Wiley.

Spunt, R. P., E. Rassin, and L. M. Epstein. 2009. "Aversive and Avoidant Indecisiveness: Roles for Regret Proneness, Maximization, and BIS/BAS Sensitivities." *Personality and Individual Differences* 47: 256–261. doi:10.1016/j.paid.2009.03.009.

Stöber, J., and J. Joormann. 2001. "Worry, Procrastination, and Perfectionism: Differentiating Amount of Worry, Pathological Worry, Anxiety and Depression." *Cognitive Therapy and Research* 25: 49–60. doi:10.1023/A:1026474715384.

Thibodeau, M. A., R. N. Carleton, P. M. McEvoy, M. J. Zvolensky, C. P. Brandt, P. A. Boelen, A. E. J. Mahoney, B. J. Deacon, and G. J. G. Asmundson. 2015. "Developing Scales Measuring Disorder-Specific Intolerance of Uncertainty (DSIU): A New Perspective on Transdiagnostic." *Journal of Anxiety Disorders* 31: 49–57. https://doi.org/10.1016/j.janxdis.2015.01.006.

Tolin, D. F., J. S. Abramowitz, B. D. Brigidi, and E. B. Foa. 2003. "Intolerance of Uncertainty in Obsessive-Compulsive Disorder." *Journal of Anxiety Disorders* 17: 233–242. http://dx.doi.org/10.1016/S0887–6185(02)00182–2.

Verhaak, P. F., S. A. Meijer, A. P. Visser, and G. Wolters. 2006. "Persistent Presentation of Medically Unexplained Symptoms in General Practice." *Family Practice* 23: 414–420.

**Melisa Robichaud, PhD,** is a clinical psychologist and cofounder of the Vancouver CBT Centre. She holds adjunct clinical faculty and clinical associate positions in psychology and psychiatry at the University of British Columbia and Simon Fraser University. Robichaud specializes in the treatment of anxiety with an emphasis on generalized anxiety disorder (GAD), and is on the scientific advisory board of AnxietyBC, as well as current president of the Canadian Association of Cognitive and Behavioural Therapies. For over a decade, she has provided workshops and training to both mental health professionals and the public on the treatment of GAD, and has published numerous book chapters and scientific articles on the subject.

**Kristin Buhr, PhD,** is a registered psychologist and director at the North Shore Stress and Anxiety Clinic in North Vancouver, BC, Canada. She is a lead consultant for AnxietyBC, where she has developed numerous self-help resources for adults, parents, and teens coping with worry and anxiety, including *MindShift*, an anxiety management app for youth and young adults. Buhr specializes in the evidence-based treatment of anxiety and mood disorders in adolescents and adults, and regularly provides training and educational workshops on mental health issues.

Foreword writer **Martin M. Antony, PhD,** is coauthor of *The Shyness and Social Anxiety Workbook* and more.